Curse of Cromwell: The Siege

Script by Dermot Poyntz

Artwork by Lee Grace

rocan press

To my daughter, Rosa Poyntz.

To my wife, Denise Grace.

Published by Moccu Press, 2010
Email: moccupress@yahoo.com
Website: www.moccupress.com

ISBN: 978-0-9566558-0-6

Printed by New Pearl River Printing, Guangzhou City, China.

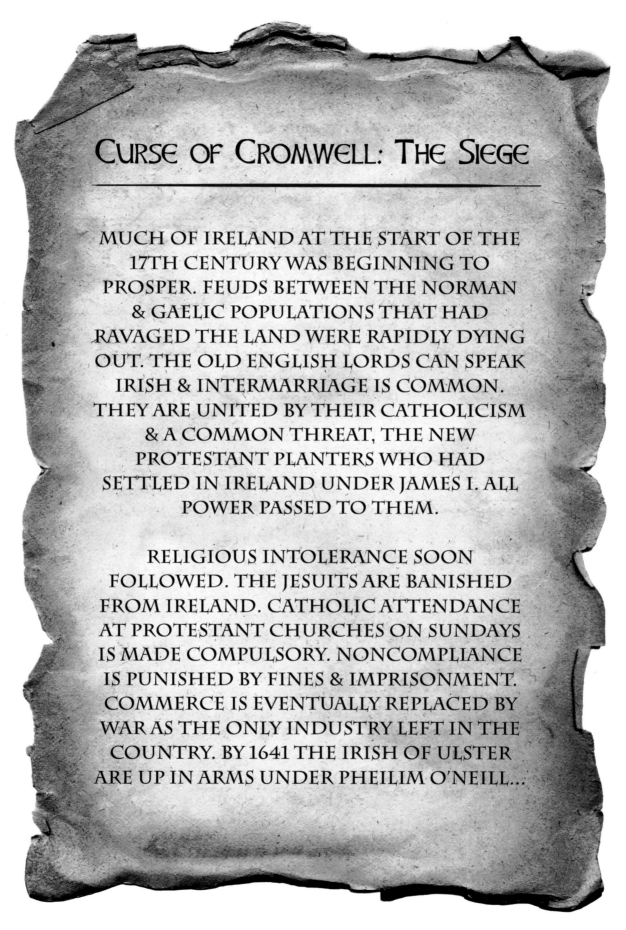

CURSE OF CROMWELL: THE SIEGE

MUCH OF IRELAND AT THE START OF THE 17TH CENTURY WAS BEGINNING TO PROSPER. FEUDS BETWEEN THE NORMAN & GAELIC POPULATIONS THAT HAD RAVAGED THE LAND WERE RAPIDLY DYING OUT. THE OLD ENGLISH LORDS CAN SPEAK IRISH & INTERMARRIAGE IS COMMON. THEY ARE UNITED BY THEIR CATHOLICISM & A COMMON THREAT, THE NEW PROTESTANT PLANTERS WHO HAD SETTLED IN IRELAND UNDER JAMES I. ALL POWER PASSED TO THEM.

RELIGIOUS INTOLERANCE SOON FOLLOWED. THE JESUITS ARE BANISHED FROM IRELAND. CATHOLIC ATTENDANCE AT PROTESTANT CHURCHES ON SUNDAYS IS MADE COMPULSORY. NONCOMPLIANCE IS PUNISHED BY FINES & IMPRISONMENT. COMMERCE IS EVENTUALLY REPLACED BY WAR AS THE ONLY INDUSTRY LEFT IN THE COUNTRY. BY 1641 THE IRISH OF ULSTER ARE UP IN ARMS UNDER PHEILIM O'NEILL...

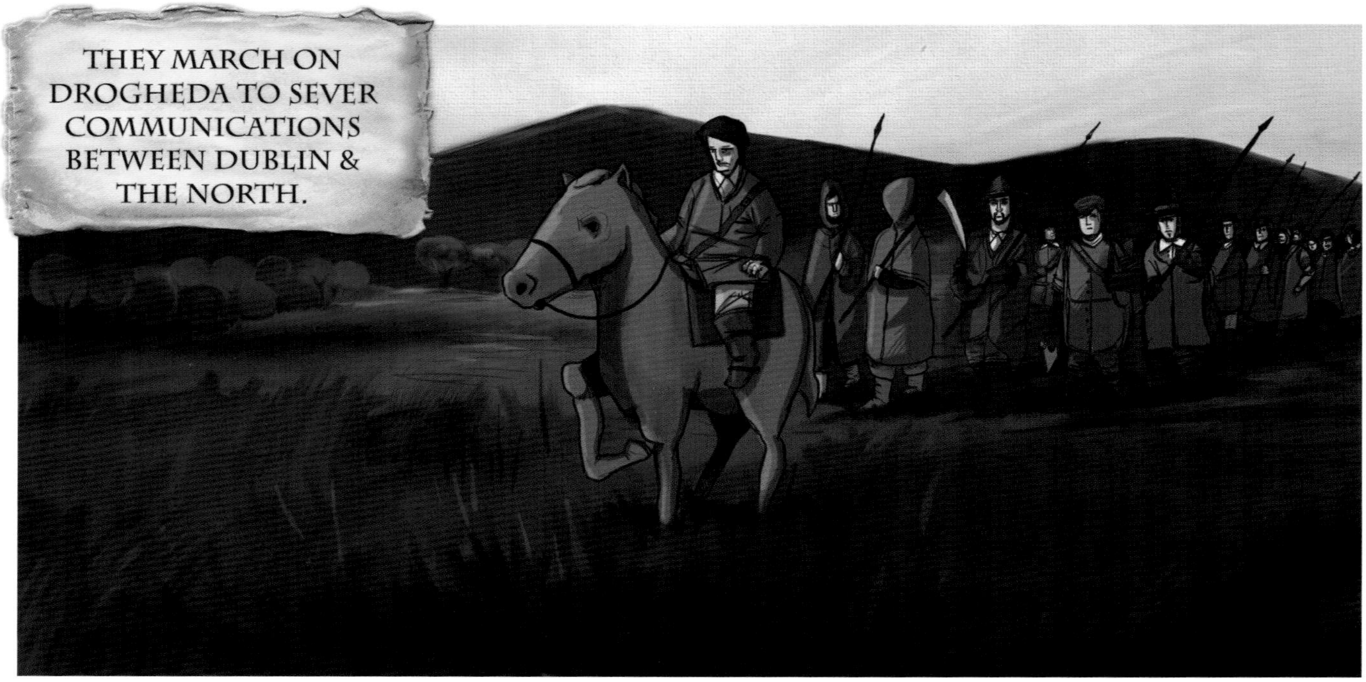
THEY MARCH ON DROGHEDA TO SEVER COMMUNICATIONS BETWEEN DUBLIN & THE NORTH.

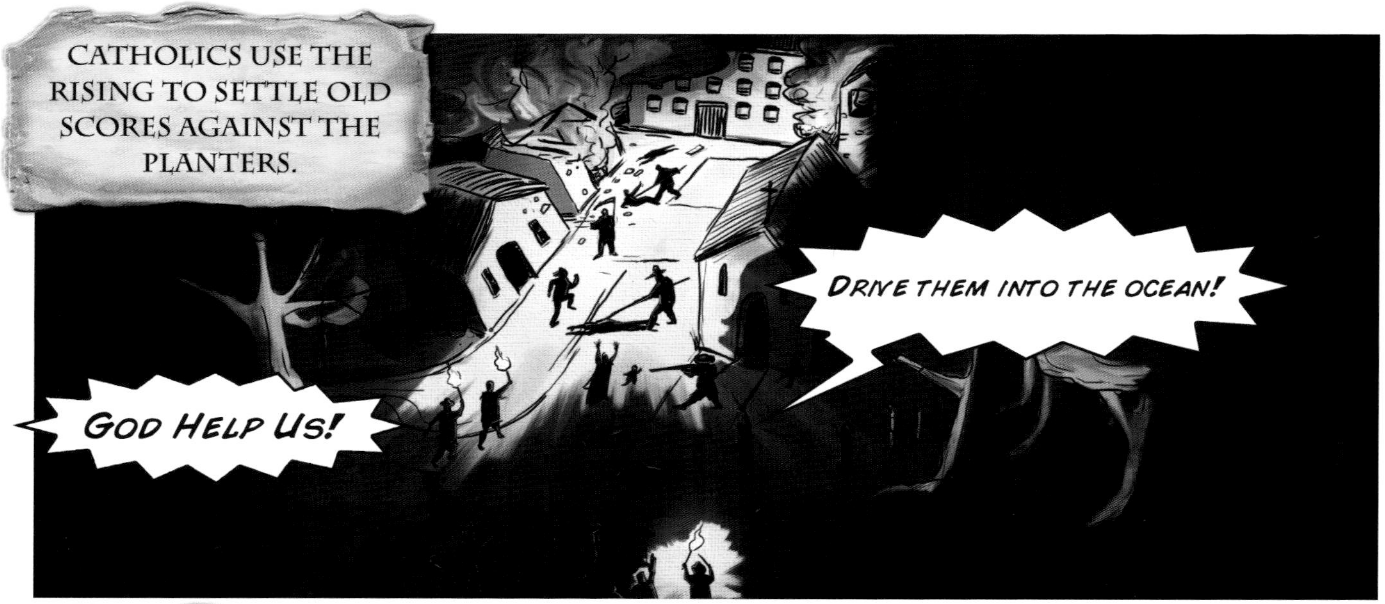
CATHOLICS USE THE RISING TO SETTLE OLD SCORES AGAINST THE PLANTERS.
GOD HELP US!
DRIVE THEM INTO THE OCEAN!

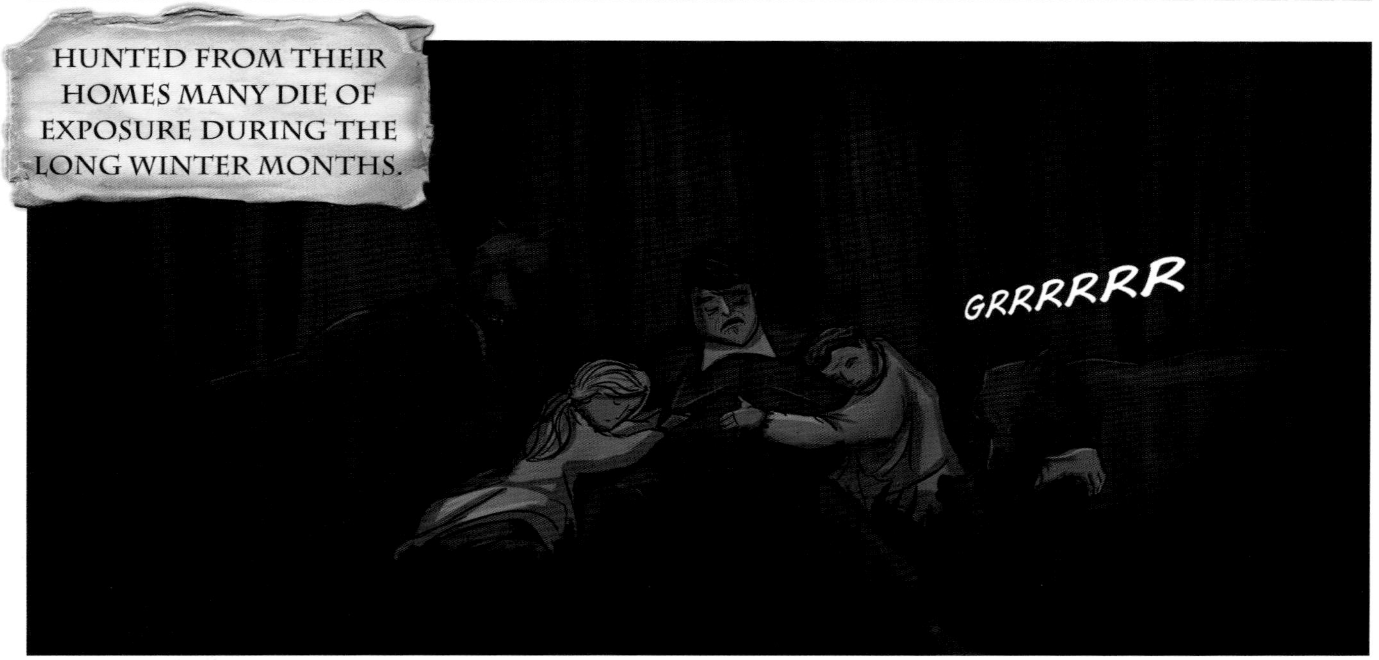
HUNTED FROM THEIR HOMES MANY DIE OF EXPOSURE DURING THE LONG WINTER MONTHS.
GRRRRRR

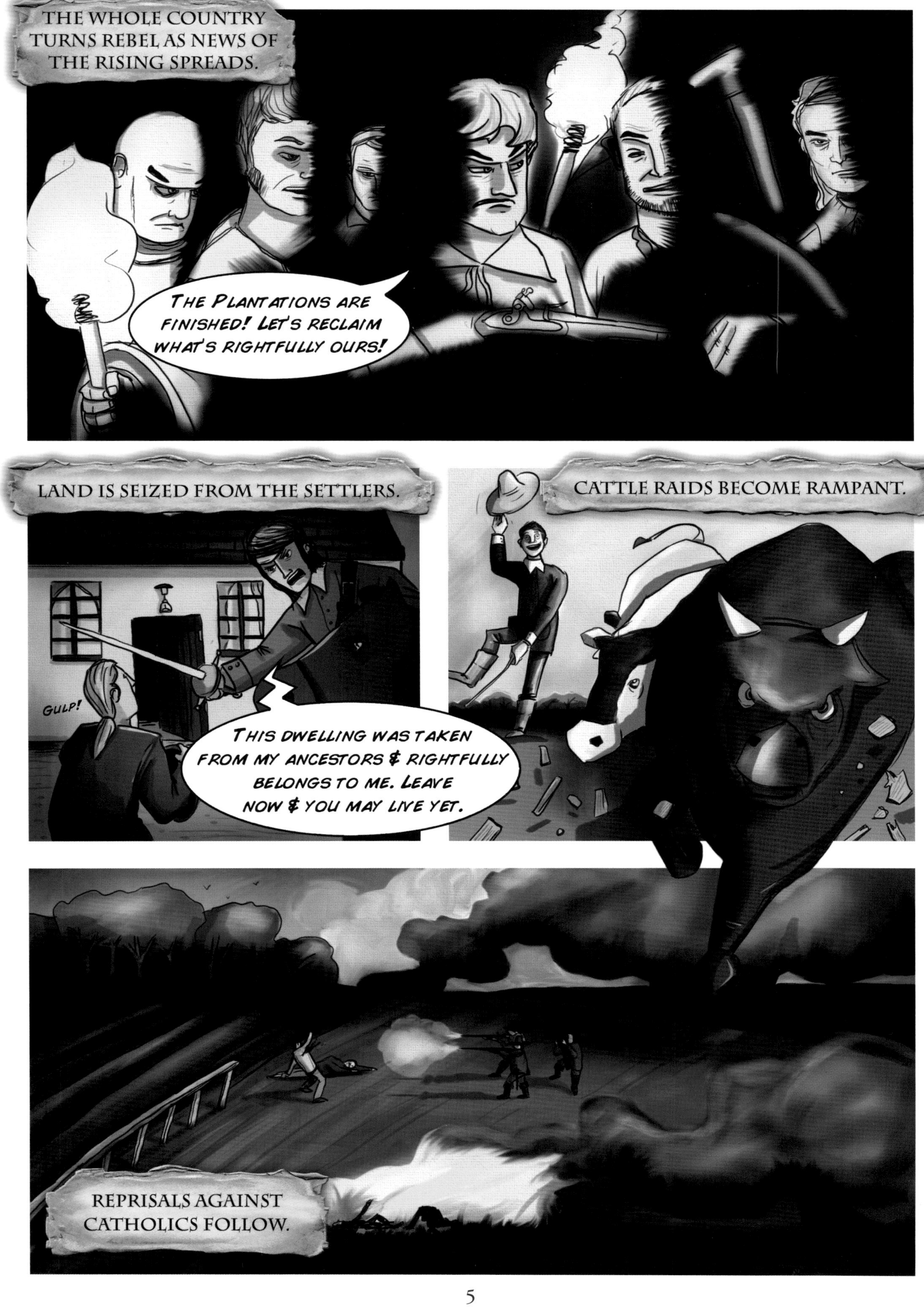
THE WHOLE COUNTRY TURNS REBEL AS NEWS OF THE RISING SPREADS.
THE PLANTATIONS ARE FINISHED! LET'S RECLAIM WHAT'S RIGHTFULLY OURS!
LAND IS SEIZED FROM THE SETTLERS.
GULP!
THIS DWELLING WAS TAKEN FROM MY ANCESTORS & RIGHTFULLY BELONGS TO ME. LEAVE NOW & YOU MAY LIVE YET.
CATTLE RAIDS BECOME RAMPANT.
REPRISALS AGAINST CATHOLICS FOLLOW.

AN ARMY FROM SCOTLAND LANDS TO PROTECT THE PURITANS & EXTINGUISH CATHOLICISM IN IRELAND.

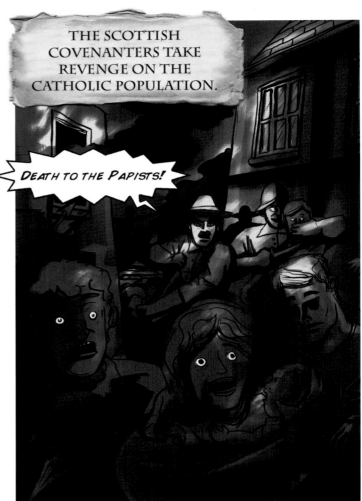

THE SCOTTISH COVENANTERS TAKE REVENGE ON THE CATHOLIC POPULATION.

DEATH TO THE PAPISTS!

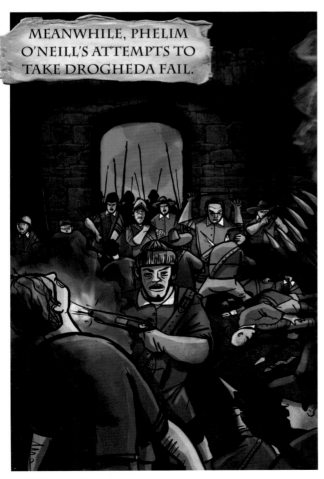

MEANWHILE, PHELIM O'NEILL'S ATTEMPTS TO TAKE DROGHEDA FAIL.

HE RETREATS IN DEFEAT TO MONAGHAN.

OWEN ROE O'NEILL ARRIVES FROM SPAIN BRINGING WITH HIM NEW HOPE...

HE RETURNS TO AN IRELAND DIVIDED INTO FOUR FACTIONS.

THE ANGLO-IRISH CATHOLICS LED BY PRESTON SUPPORT THE KING, & FIGHT FOR RELIGIOUS TOLERANCE.

ENGLISH & SCOTTISH PURITANS UNDER MONROE.

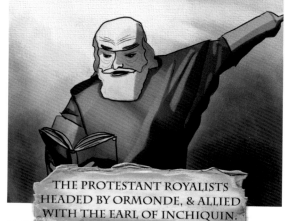

THE PROTESTANT ROYALISTS HEADED BY ORMONDE, & ALLIED WITH THE EARL OF INCHIQUIN.

THE GAELIC IRISH WHO WANT COMPLETE SEPARATION FROM ENGLAND.

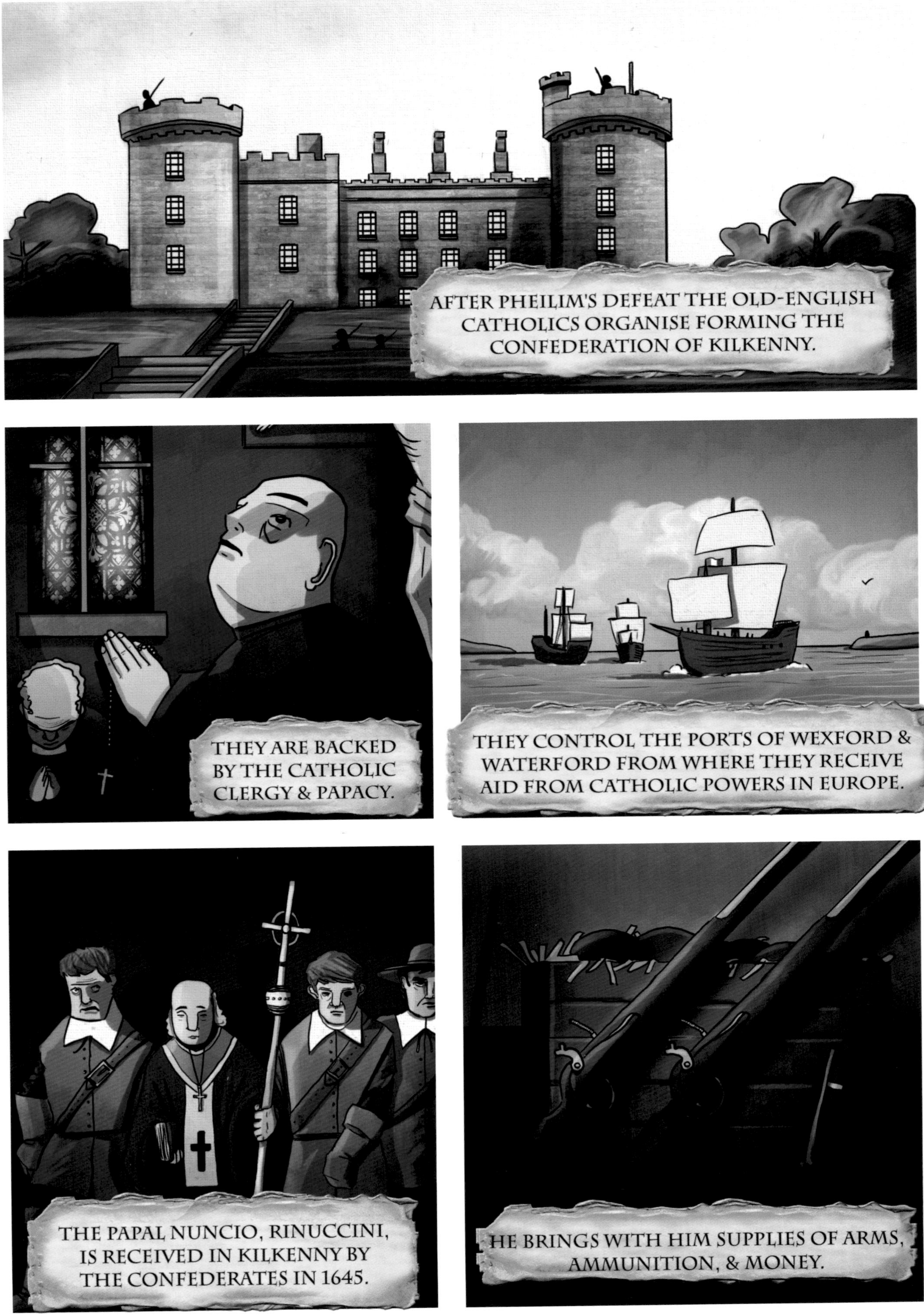
AFTER PHEILIM'S DEFEAT THE OLD-ENGLISH CATHOLICS ORGANISE FORMING THE CONFEDERATION OF KILKENNY.
THEY ARE BACKED BY THE CATHOLIC CLERGY & PAPACY.
THEY CONTROL THE PORTS OF WEXFORD & WATERFORD FROM WHERE THEY RECEIVE AID FROM CATHOLIC POWERS IN EUROPE.
THE PAPAL NUNCIO, RINUCCINI, IS RECEIVED IN KILKENNY BY THE CONFEDERATES IN 1645.
HE BRINGS WITH HIM SUPPLIES OF ARMS, AMMUNITION, & MONEY.

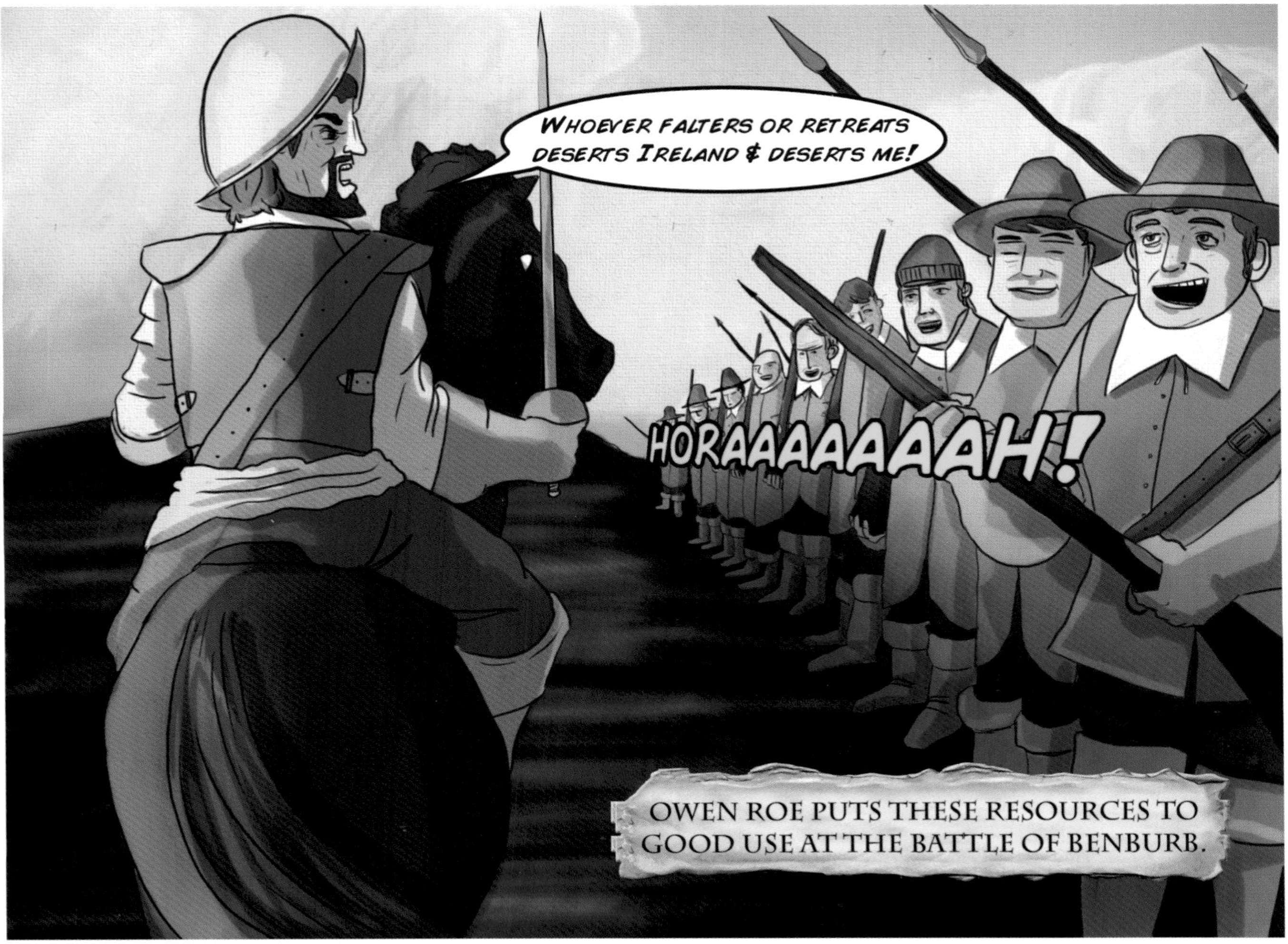
WHOEVER FALTERS OR RETREATS DESERTS IRELAND & DESERTS ME!
HORAAAAAAAAH!
OWEN ROE PUTS THESE RESOURCES TO GOOD USE AT THE BATTLE OF BENBURB.

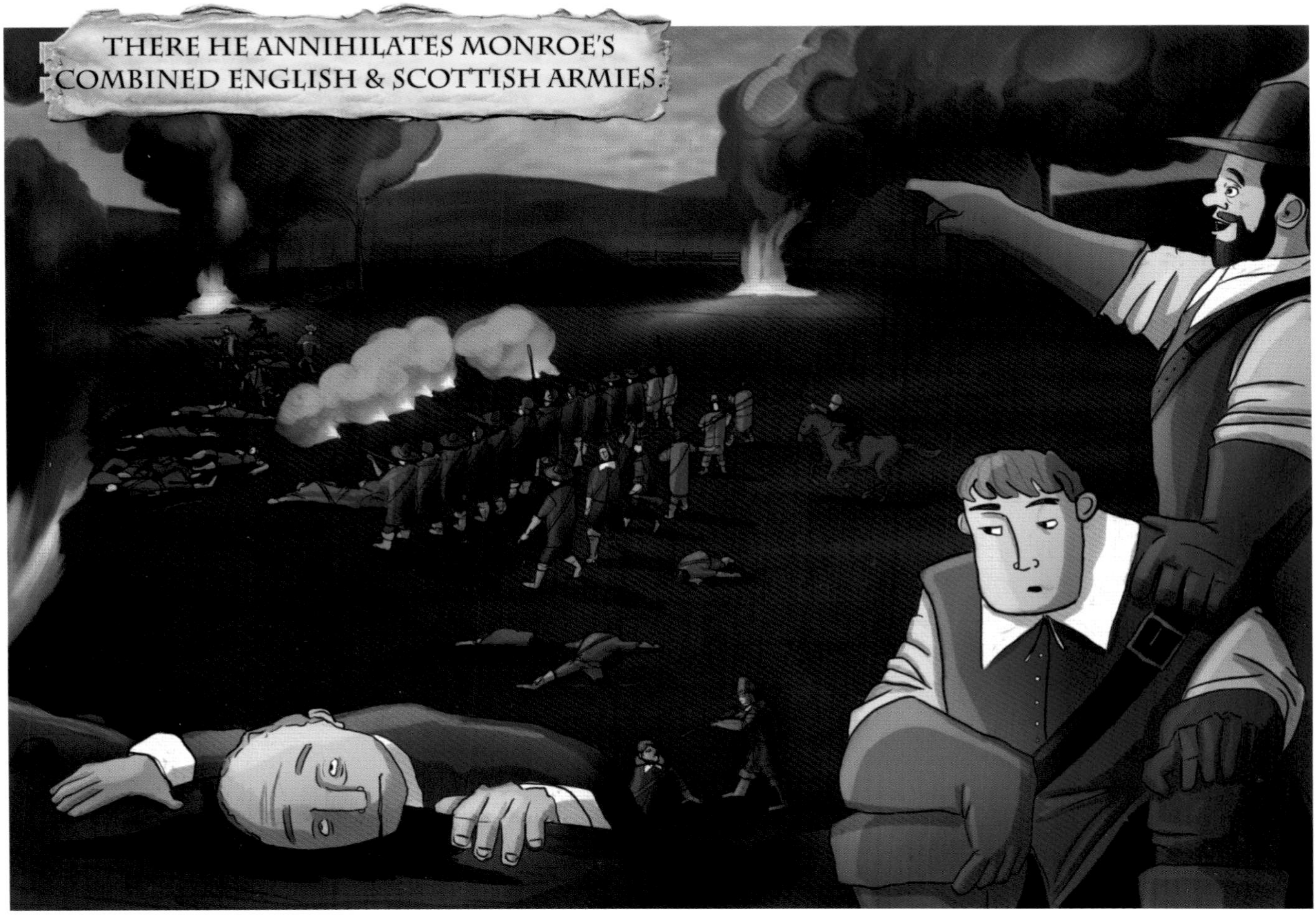
THERE HE ANNIHILATES MONROE'S COMBINED ENGLISH & SCOTTISH ARMIES.

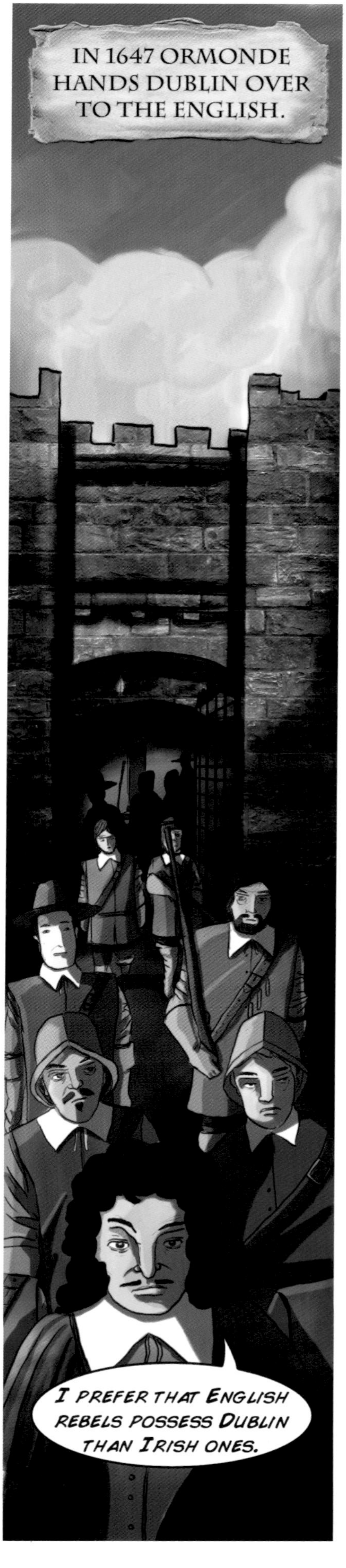
IN 1647 ORMONDE HANDS DUBLIN OVER TO THE ENGLISH.
I PREFER THAT ENGLISH REBELS POSSESS DUBLIN THAN IRISH ONES.

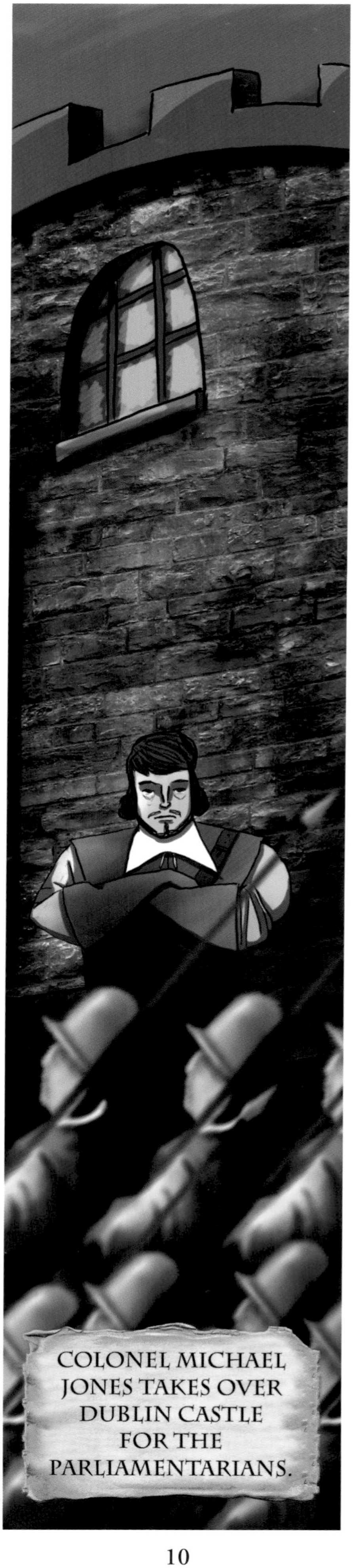
COLONEL MICHAEL JONES TAKES OVER DUBLIN CASTLE FOR THE PARLIAMENTARIANS.

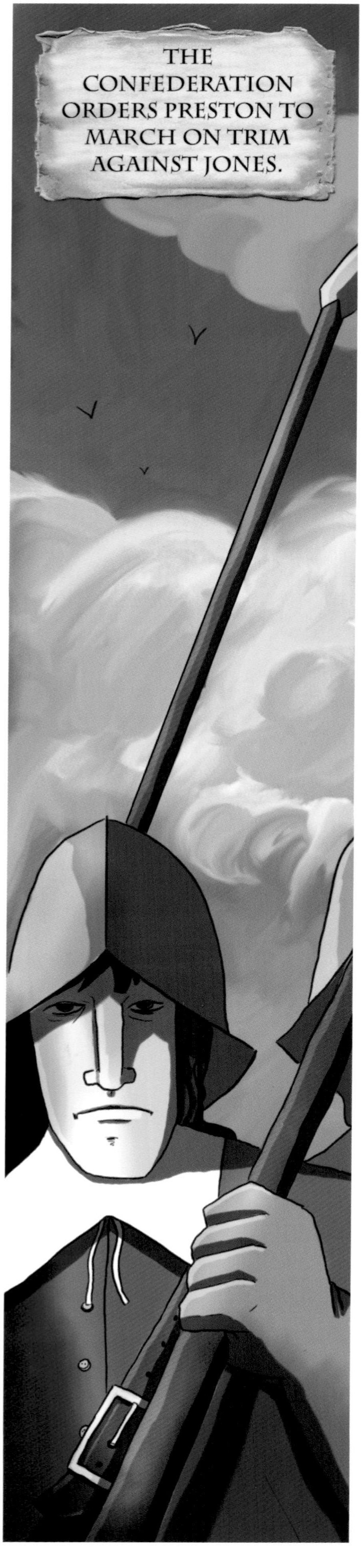
THE CONFEDERATION ORDERS PRESTON TO MARCH ON TRIM AGAINST JONES.

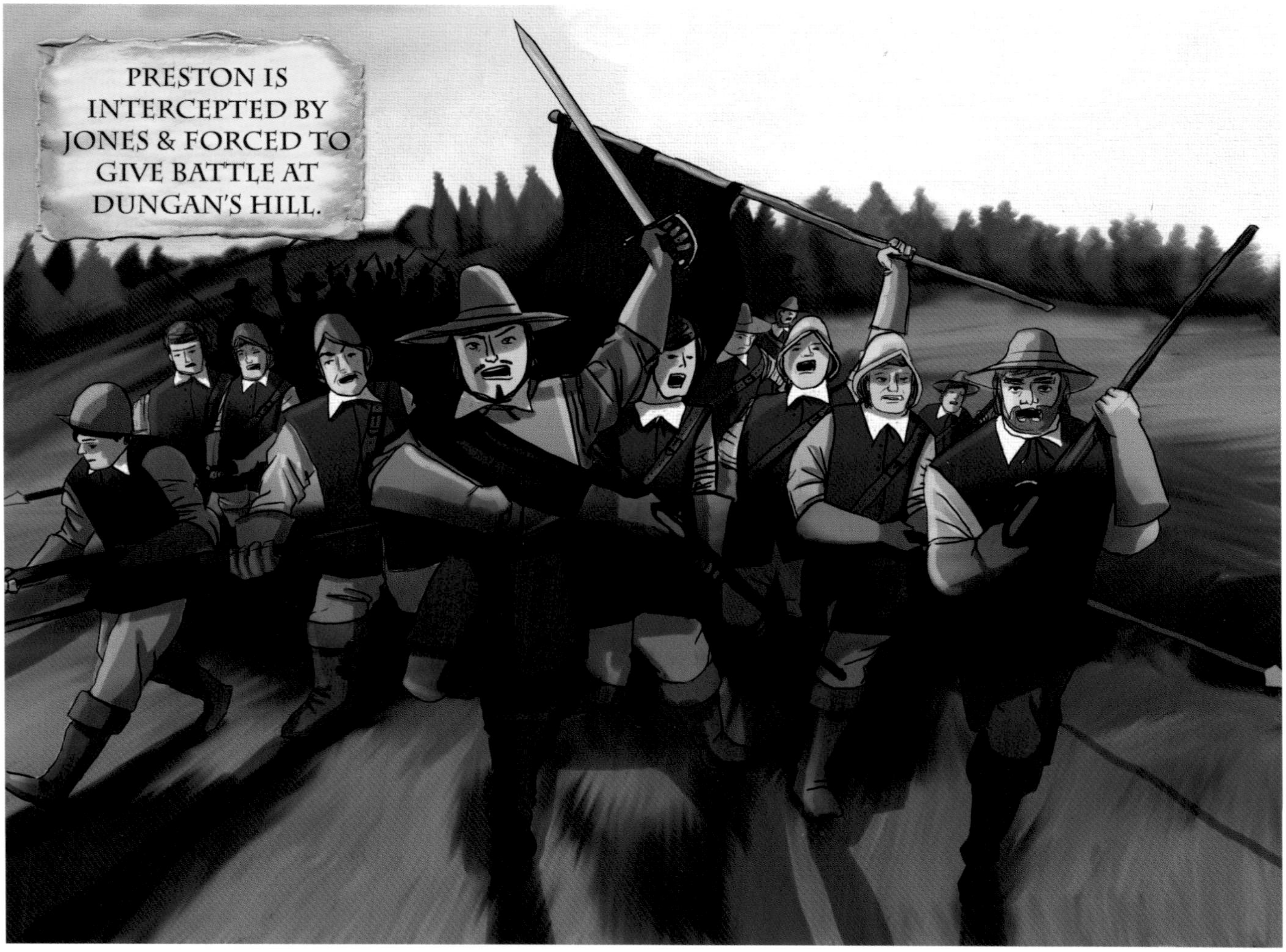
PRESTON IS INTERCEPTED BY JONES & FORCED TO GIVE BATTLE AT DUNGAN'S HILL.

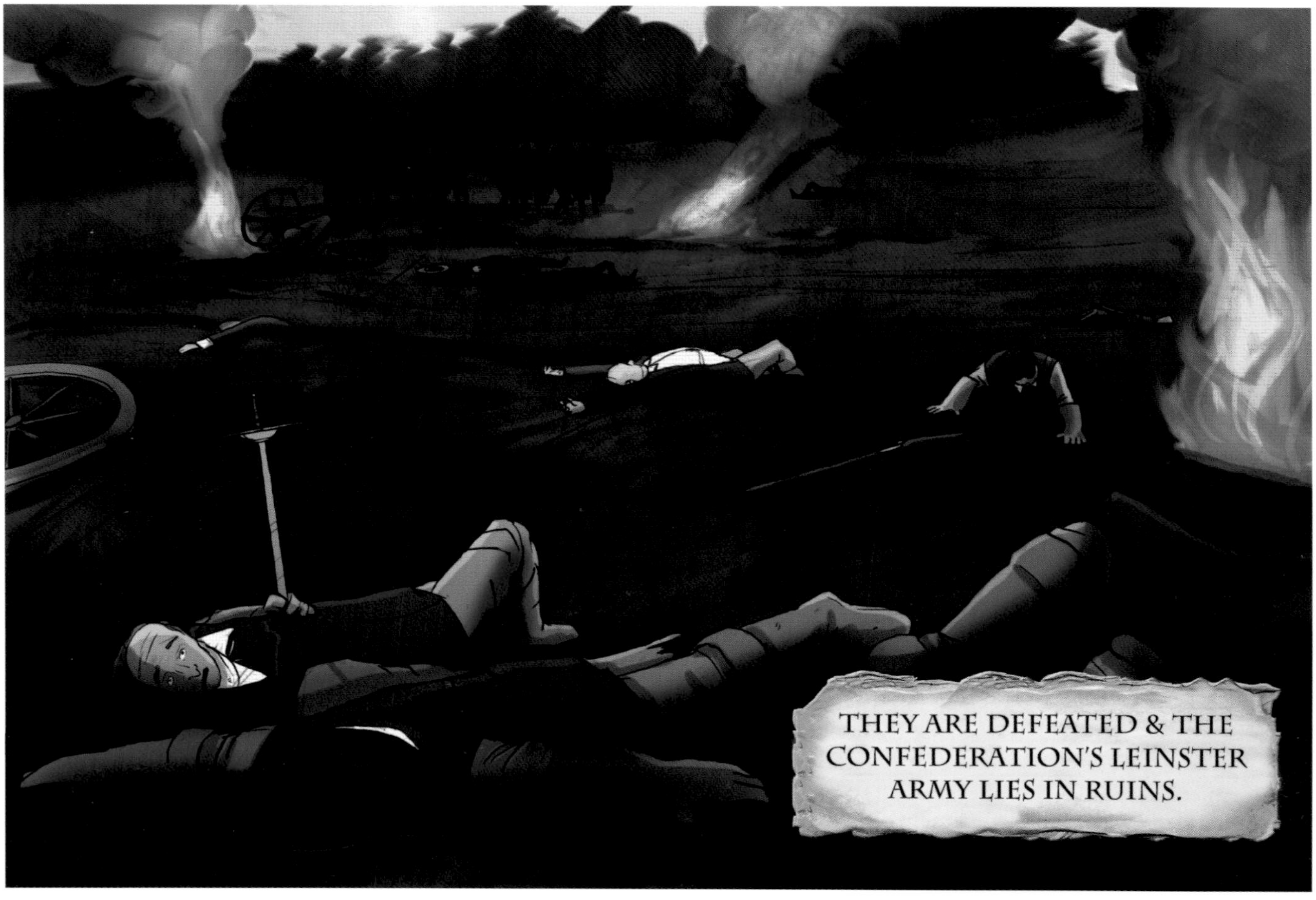
THEY ARE DEFEATED & THE CONFEDERATION'S LEINSTER ARMY LIES IN RUINS.

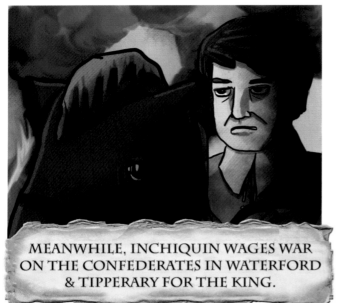

MEANWHILE, INCHIQUIN WAGES WAR ON THE CONFEDERATES IN WATERFORD & TIPPERARY FOR THE KING.
AT CARRICK ON SUIR HE EXECUTES PRISONERS TAKEN IN A SKIRMISH.
INCHIQUIN DEFECTS TO THE PARLIAMENTARIAN SIDE WHEN OFFERED THE PRESIDENCY OF MUNSTER.
DON'T FIRE! WE SURRENDER!
HE MARCHES ON CAHIR & TAKES THE CASTLE IN A DAY.
STORM THE TOWN! GIVE NO QUARTER!
INCHIQUIN ATTACKS CASHEL NEXT.
THE GARRISON ARE MASSACRED MERCILESSLY.

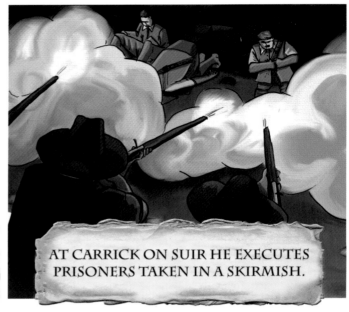

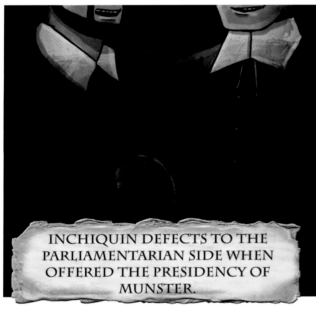

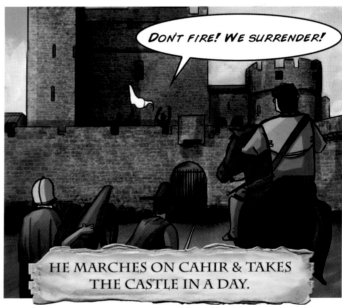

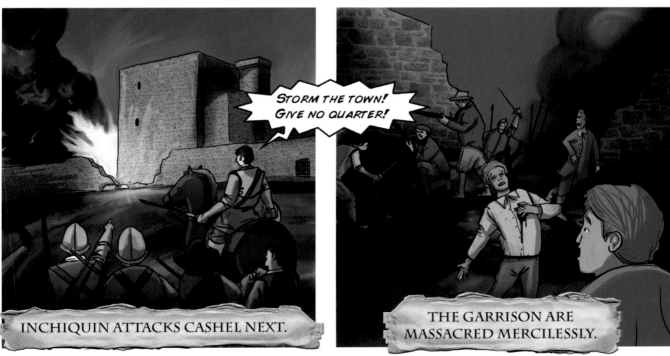

THE TOWNSPEOPLE ARE SLAIN INDISCRIMINATELY.

AAAAAHH

THEY FLEE TO THE CATHEDRAL FOR SANCTUARY.

INCHIQUIN'S SOLDIERS SURROUND THEM.

OPEN FIRE!

THEN SHOWER THE CATHEDRAL WITH LEAD.

THE SOLDIERS STORM IN & FINISH THE BUSINESS WITH COLD STEEL.

PLEASE, HAVE MERCY!

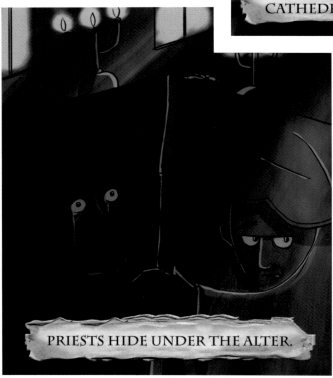

PRIESTS HIDE UNDER THE ALTER.

THEY ARE DRAGGED OUTSIDE & EXECUTED.

OUR FATHER, WHO ART IN HEAVEN...

13

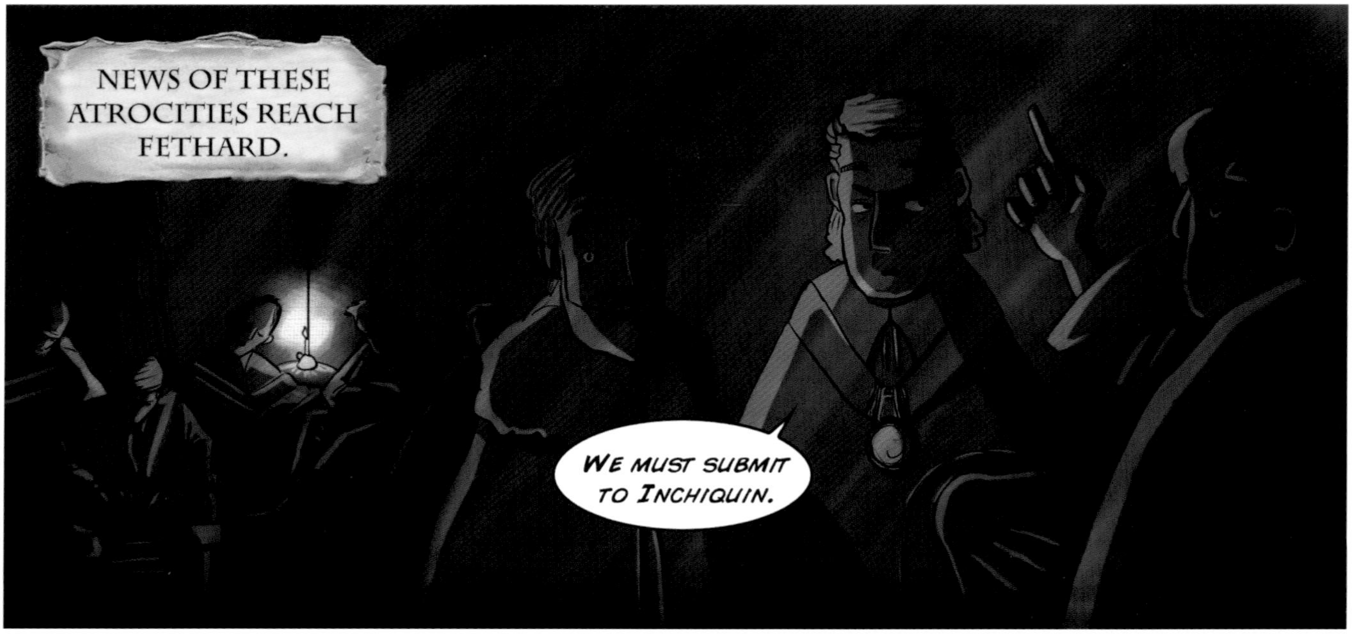
NEWS OF THESE ATROCITIES REACH FETHARD.
WE MUST SUBMIT TO INCHIQUIN.

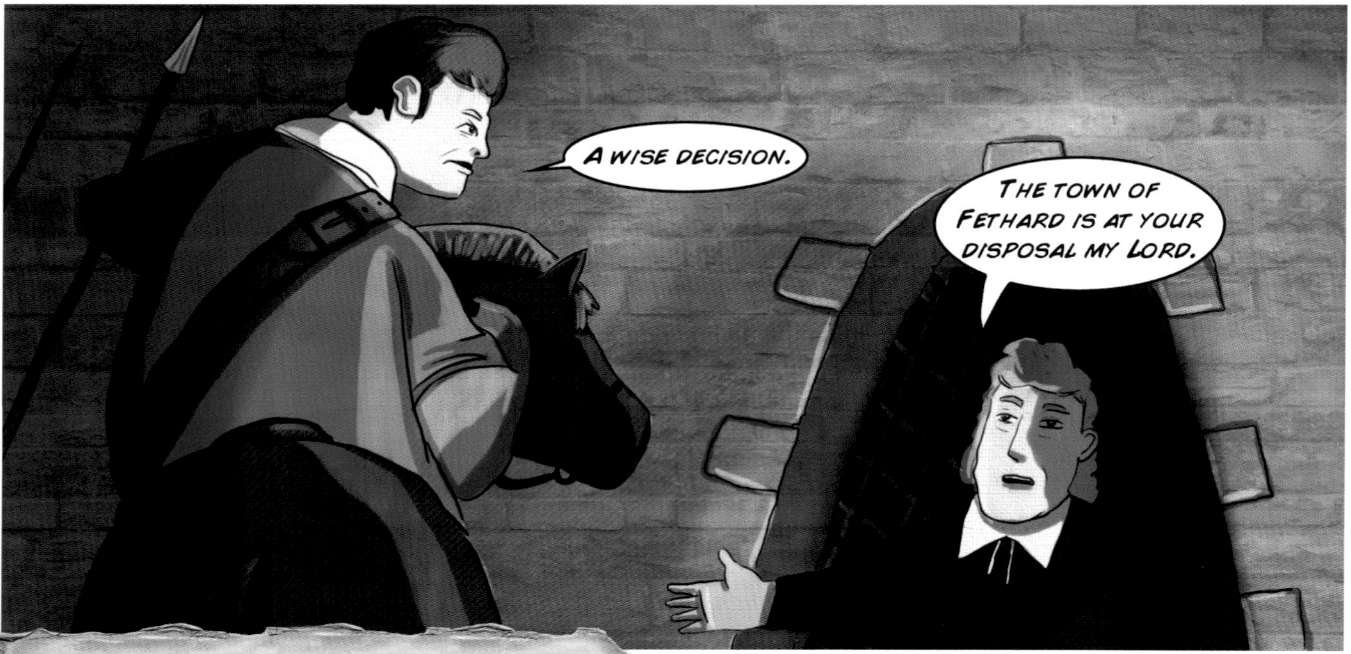
A WISE DECISION.
THE TOWN OF FETHARD IS AT YOUR DISPOSAL MY LORD.

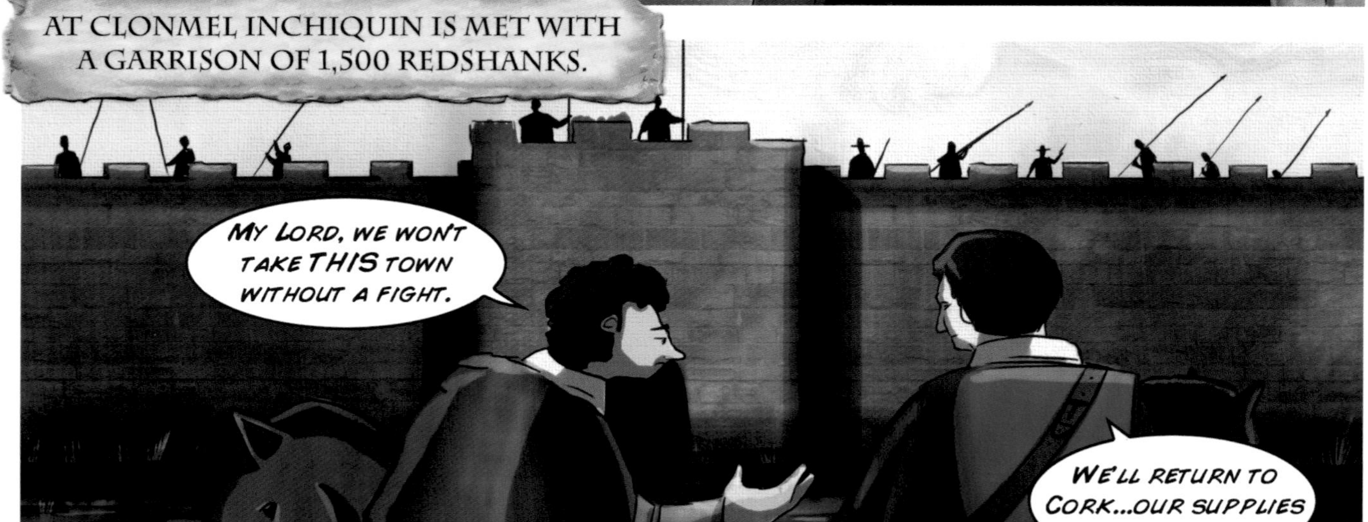
AT CLONMEL INCHIQUIN IS MET WITH A GARRISON OF 1,500 REDSHANKS.
MY LORD, WE WONT TAKE THIS TOWN WITHOUT A FIGHT.
WE'LL RETURN TO CORK...OUR SUPPLIES ARE SPENT.

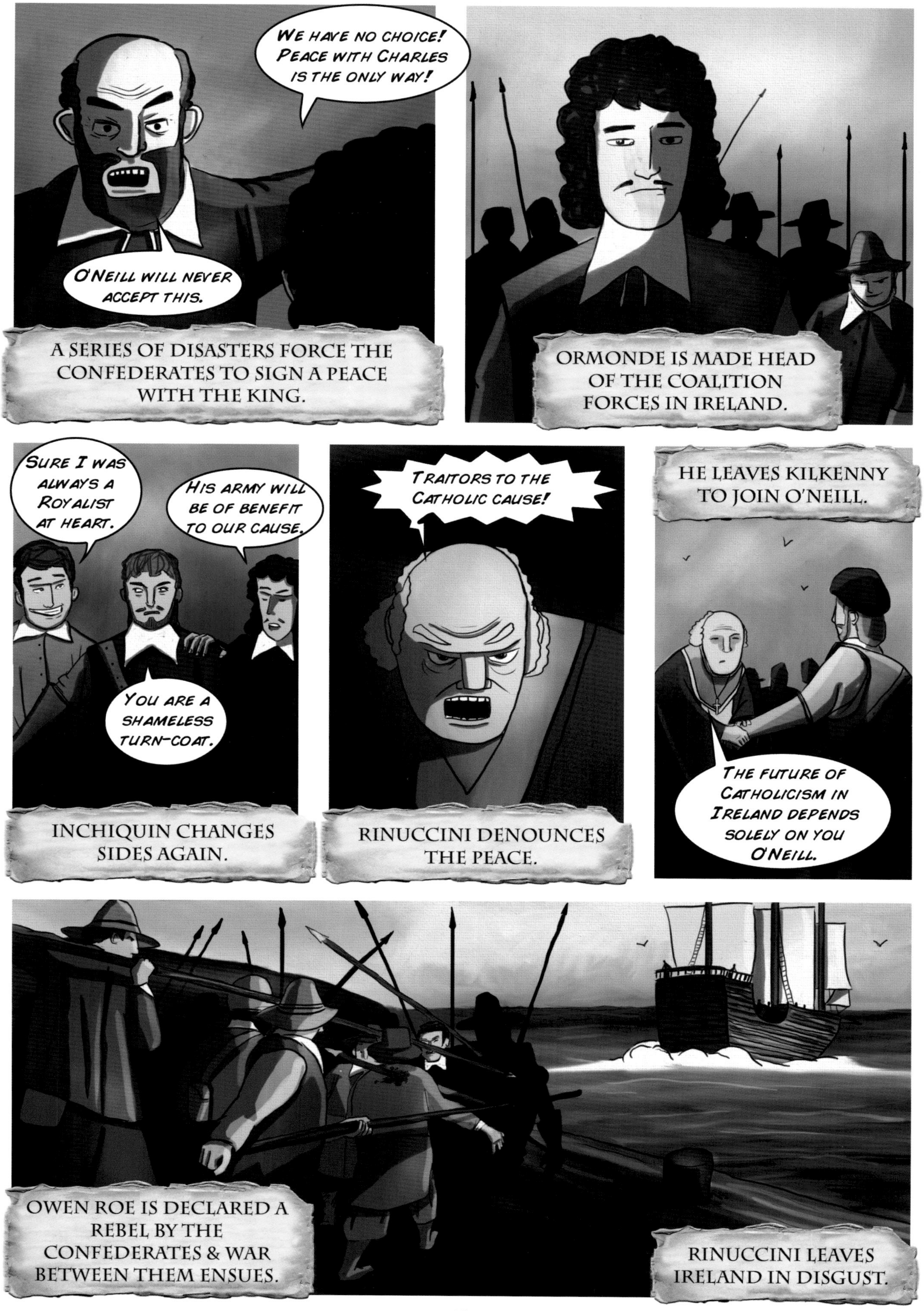
WE HAVE NO CHOICE! PEACE WITH CHARLES IS THE ONLY WAY!
O'NEILL WILL NEVER ACCEPT THIS.
A SERIES OF DISASTERS FORCE THE CONFEDERATES TO SIGN A PEACE WITH THE KING.
ORMONDE IS MADE HEAD OF THE COALITION FORCES IN IRELAND.
SURE I WAS ALWAYS A ROYALIST AT HEART.
HIS ARMY WILL BE OF BENEFIT TO OUR CAUSE.
YOU ARE A SHAMELESS TURN-COAT.
INCHIQUIN CHANGES SIDES AGAIN.
TRAITORS TO THE CATHOLIC CAUSE!
RINUCCINI DENOUNCES THE PEACE.
HE LEAVES KILKENNY TO JOIN O'NEILL.
THE FUTURE OF CATHOLICISM IN IRELAND DEPENDS SOLELY ON YOU O'NEILL.
OWEN ROE IS DECLARED A REBEL BY THE CONFEDERATES & WAR BETWEEN THEM ENSUES.
RINUCCINI LEAVES IRELAND IN DISGUST.

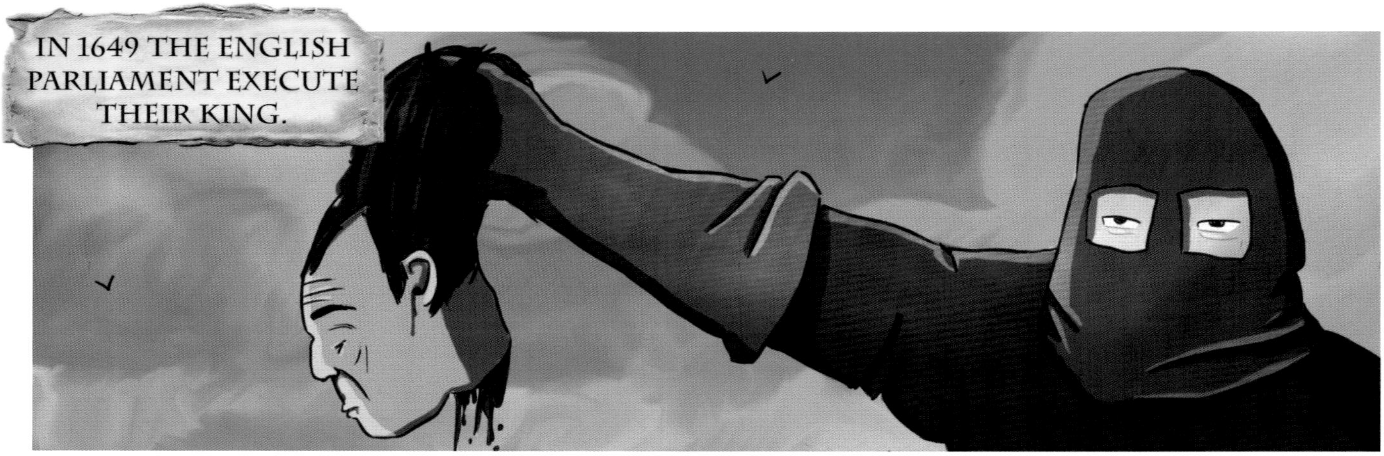
IN 1649 THE ENGLISH PARLIAMENT EXECUTE THEIR KING.

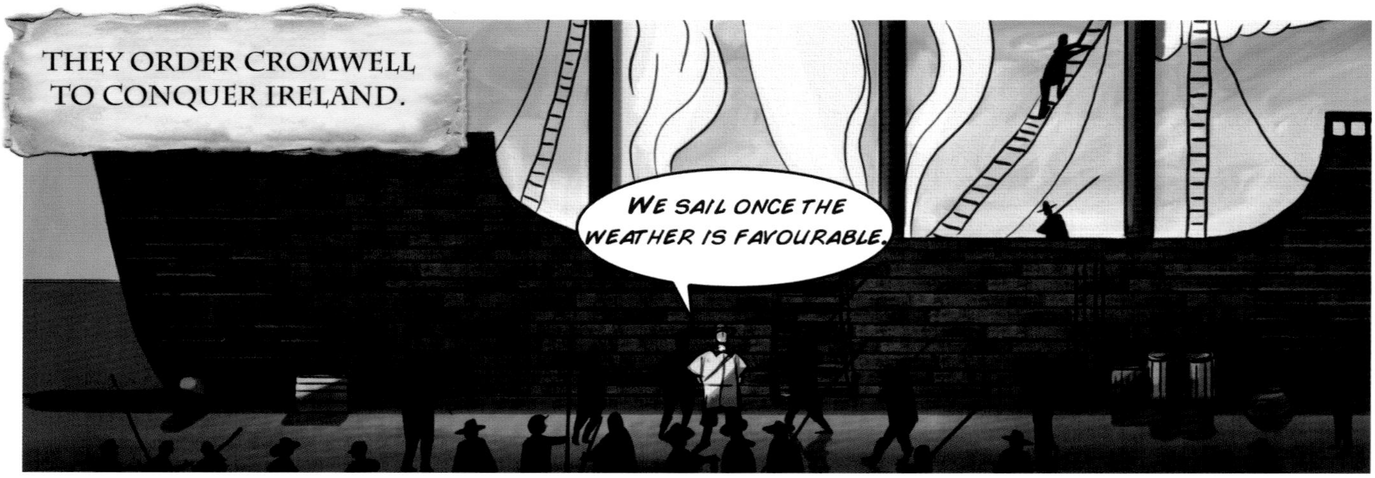
THEY ORDER CROMWELL TO CONQUER IRELAND.
WE SAIL ONCE THE WEATHER IS FAVOURABLE.

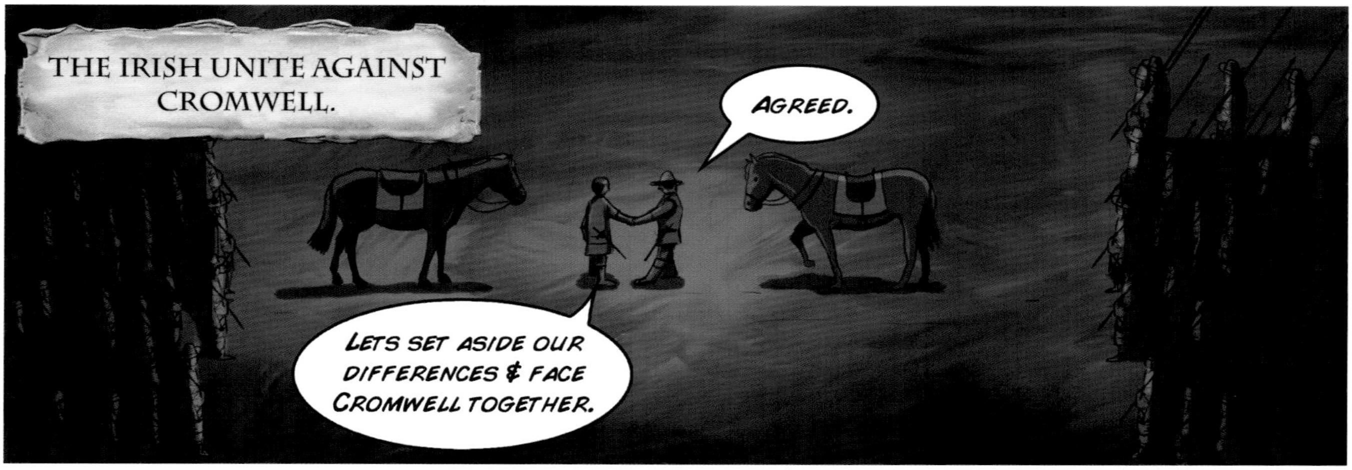
THE IRISH UNITE AGAINST CROMWELL.
LETS SET ASIDE OUR DIFFERENCES & FACE CROMWELL TOGETHER.
AGREED.

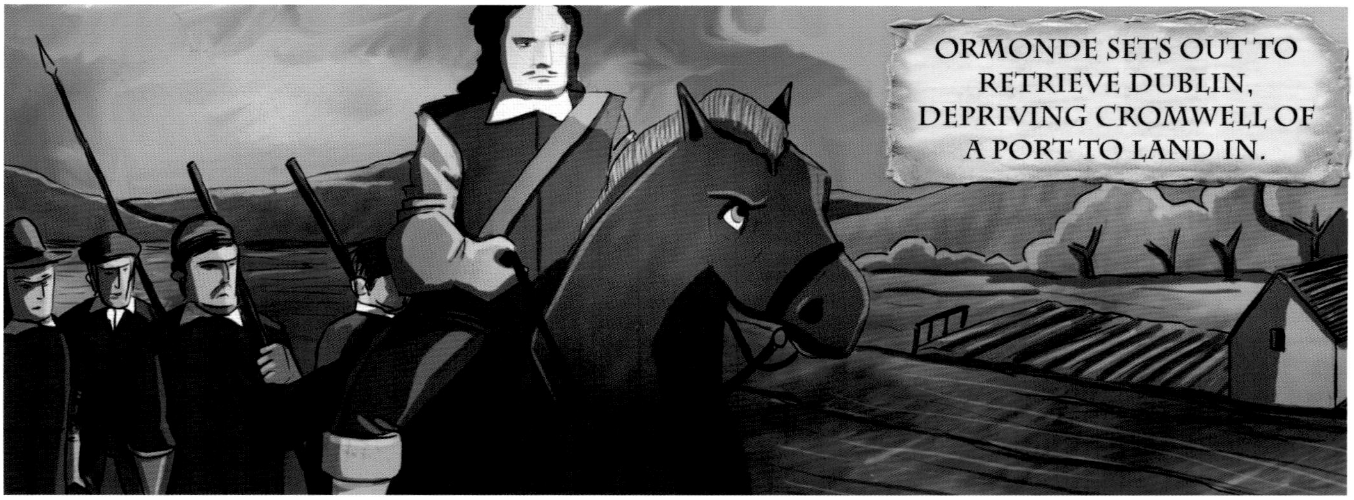
ORMONDE SETS OUT TO RETRIEVE DUBLIN, DEPRIVING CROMWELL OF A PORT TO LAND IN.

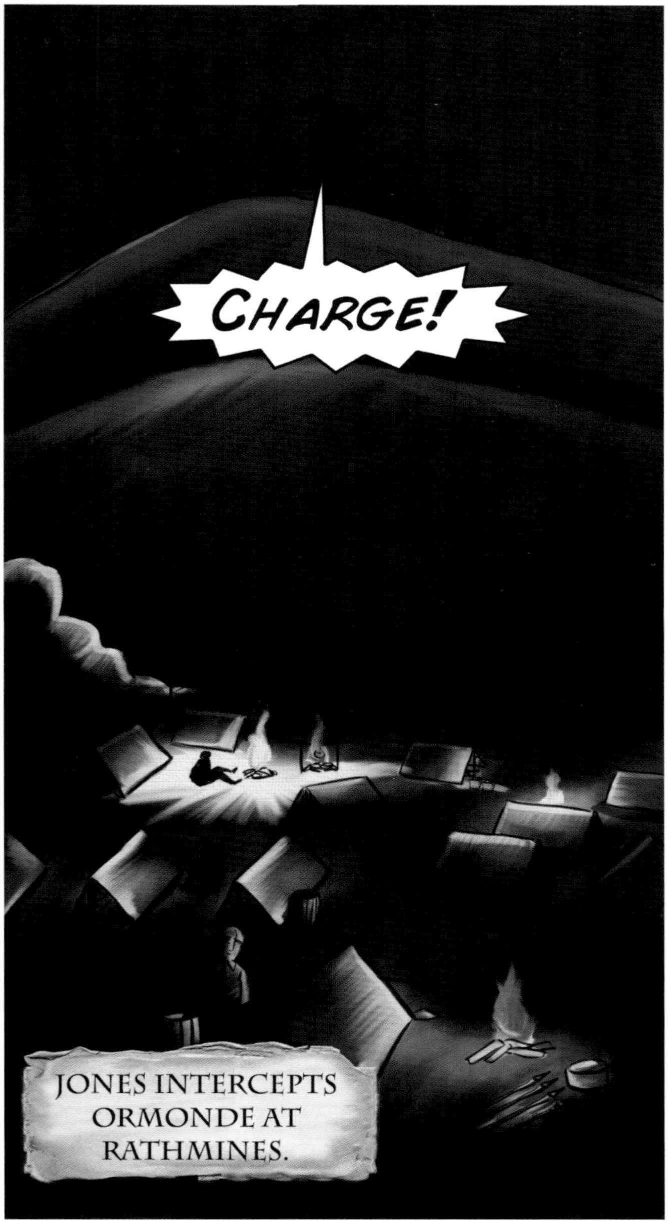
CHARGE!
JONES INTERCEPTS ORMONDE AT RATHMINES.

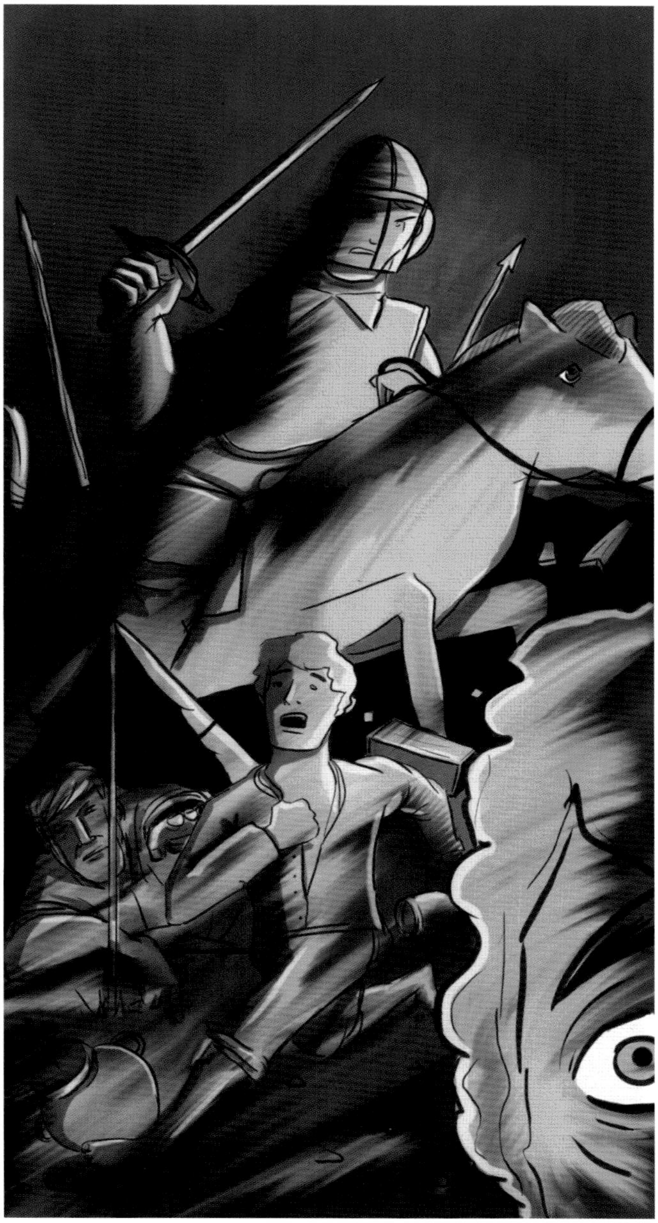

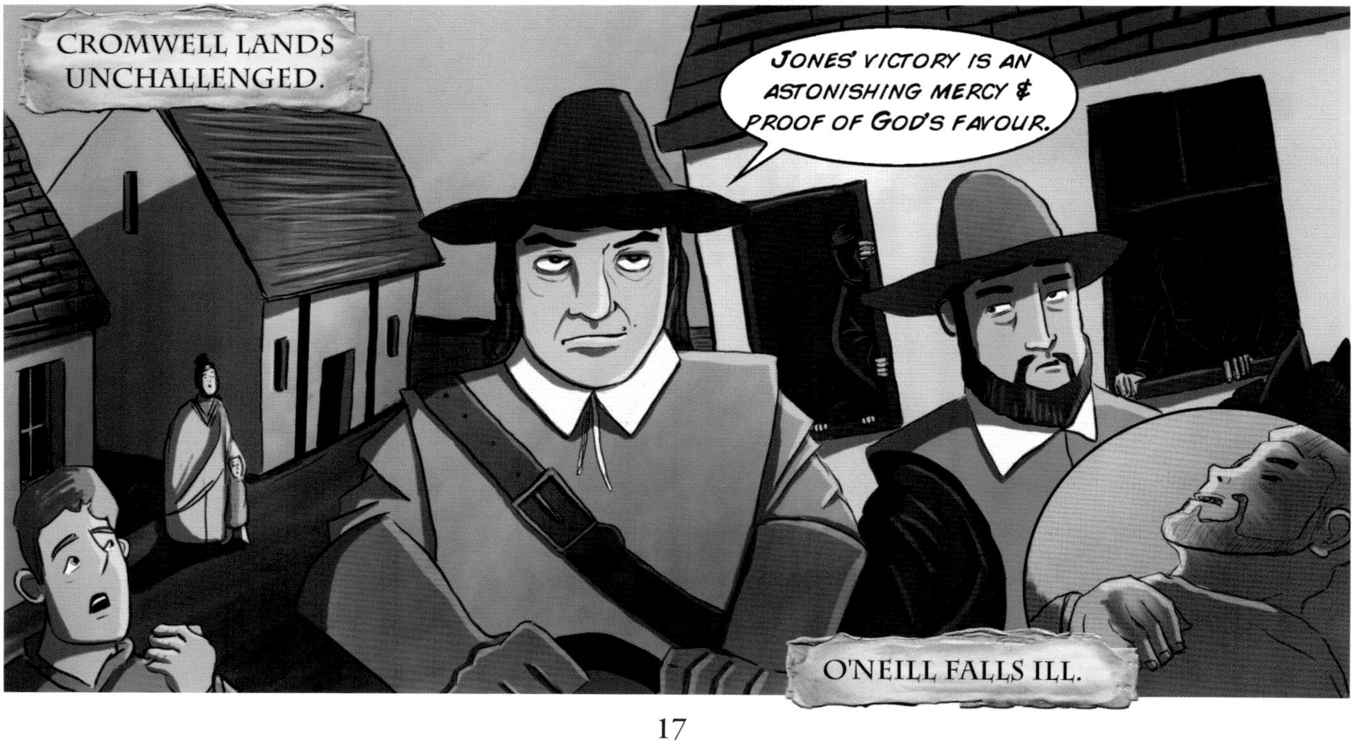
CROMWELL LANDS UNCHALLENGED.
JONES' VICTORY IS AN ASTONISHING MERCY & PROOF OF GOD'S FAVOUR.
O'NEILL FALLS ILL.

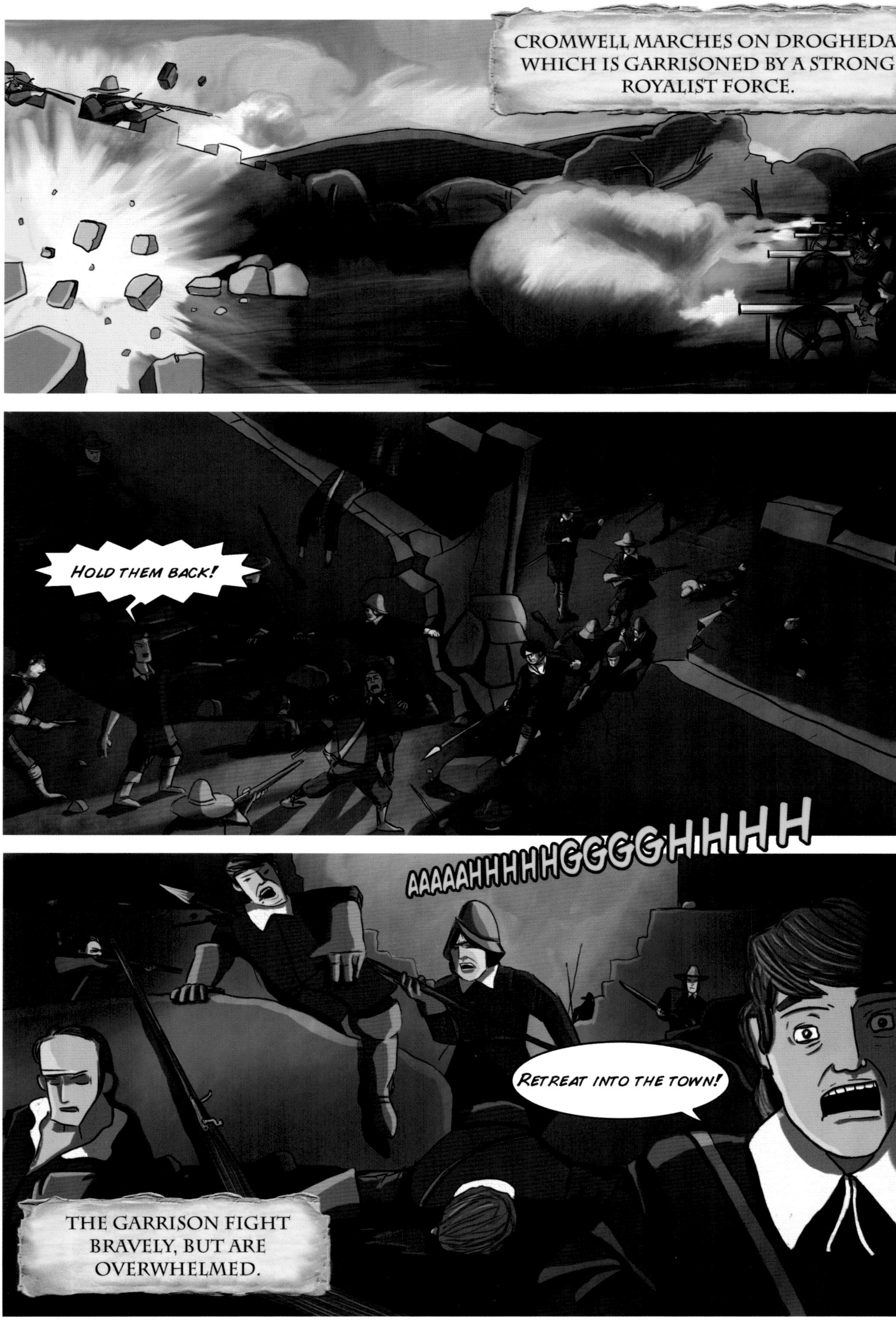

CROMWELL MARCHES ON DROGHEDA, WHICH IS GARRISONED BY A STRONG ROYALIST FORCE.
HOLD THEM BACK!
AAAAAHHHHHGGGGHHHHH
RETREAT INTO THE TOWN!
THE GARRISON FIGHT BRAVELY, BUT ARE OVERWHELMED.

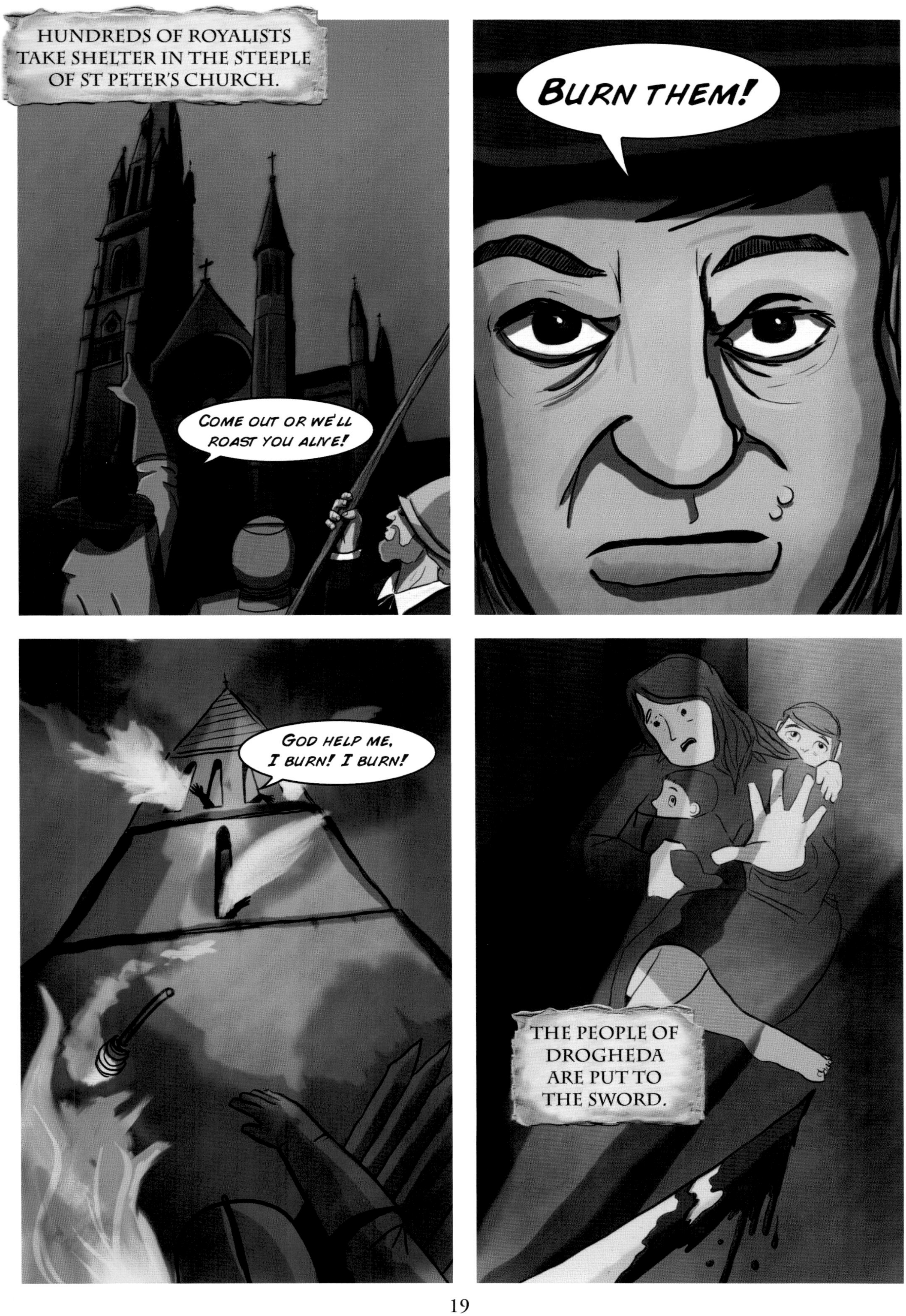
HUNDREDS OF ROYALISTS TAKE SHELTER IN THE STEEPLE OF ST PETER'S CHURCH.
COME OUT OR WE'LL ROAST YOU ALIVE!
BURN THEM!
GOD HELP ME, I BURN! I BURN!
THE PEOPLE OF DROGHEDA ARE PUT TO THE SWORD.

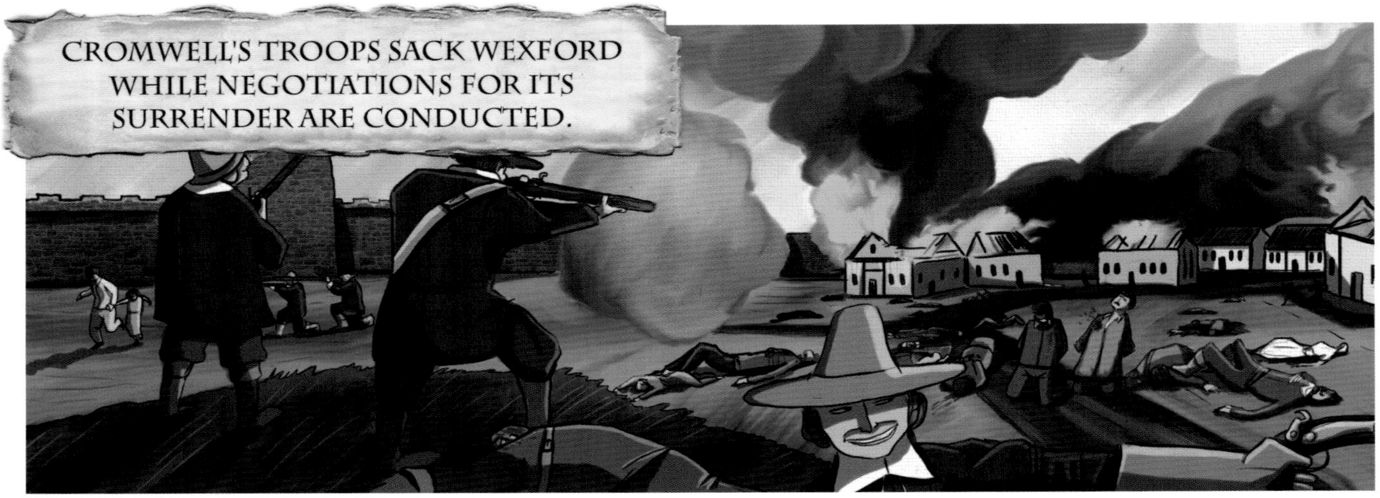
CROMWELL'S TROOPS SACK WEXFORD WHILE NEGOTIATIONS FOR ITS SURRENDER ARE CONDUCTED.

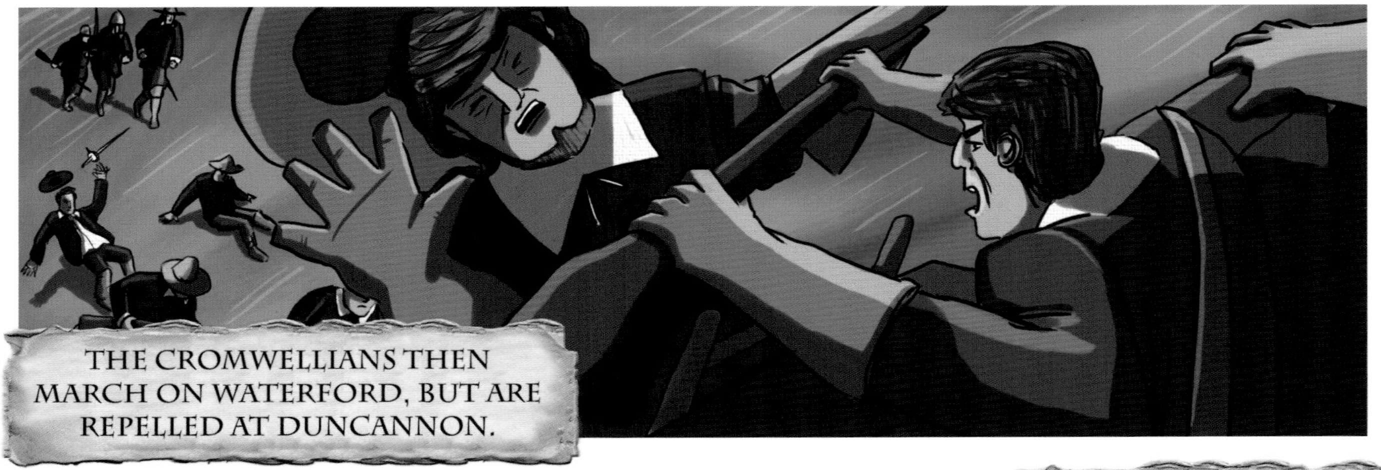
THE CROMWELLIANS THEN MARCH ON WATERFORD, BUT ARE REPELLED AT DUNCANNON.

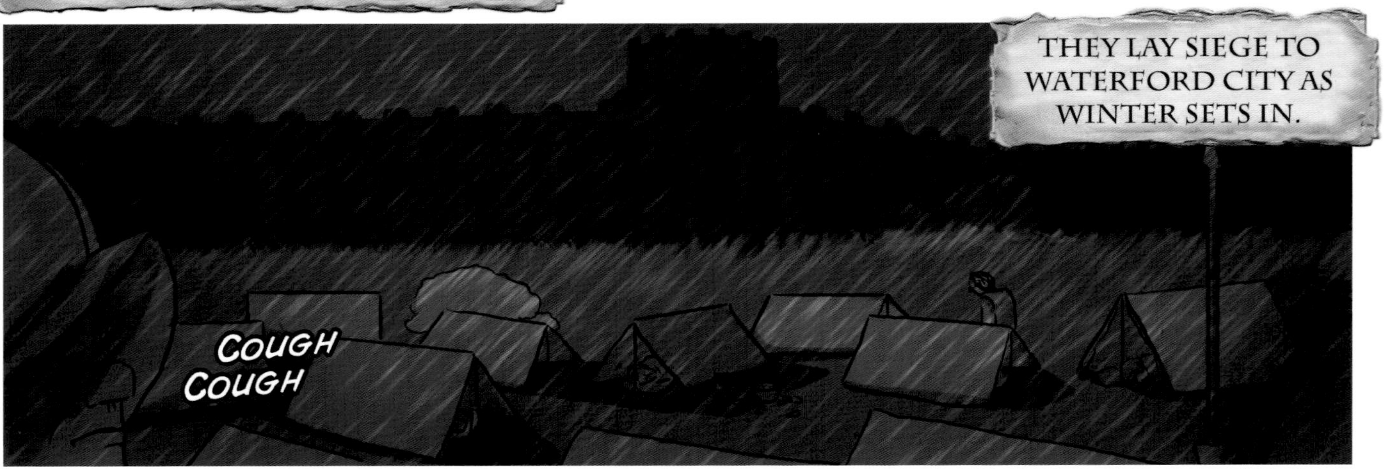
THEY LAY SIEGE TO WATERFORD CITY AS WINTER SETS IN.
COUGH COUGH

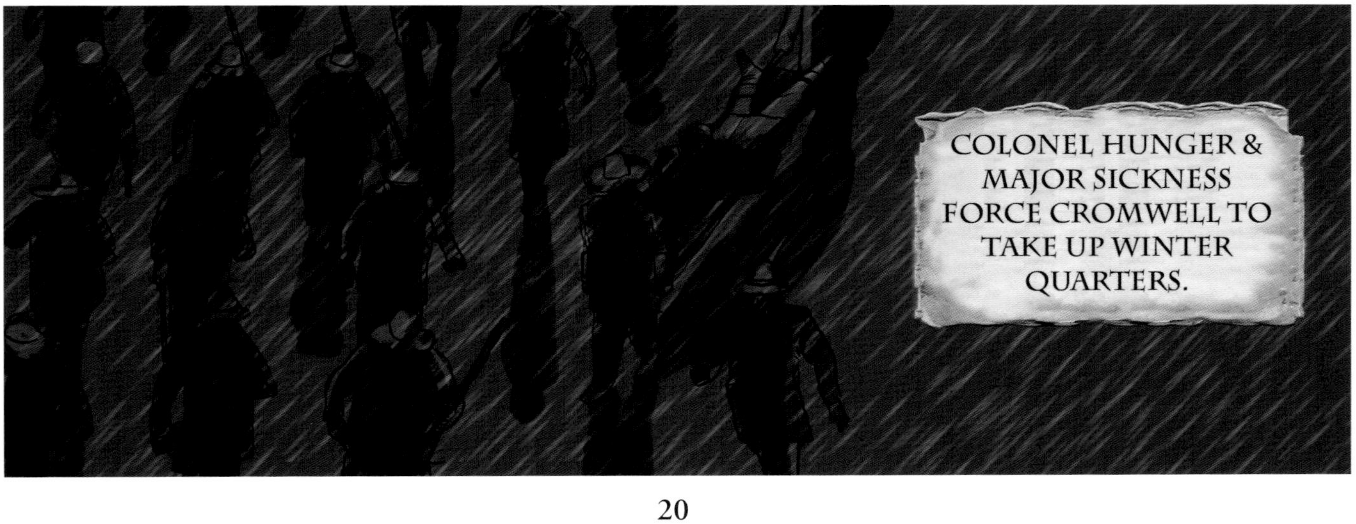
COLONEL HUNGER & MAJOR SICKNESS FORCE CROMWELL TO TAKE UP WINTER QUARTERS.

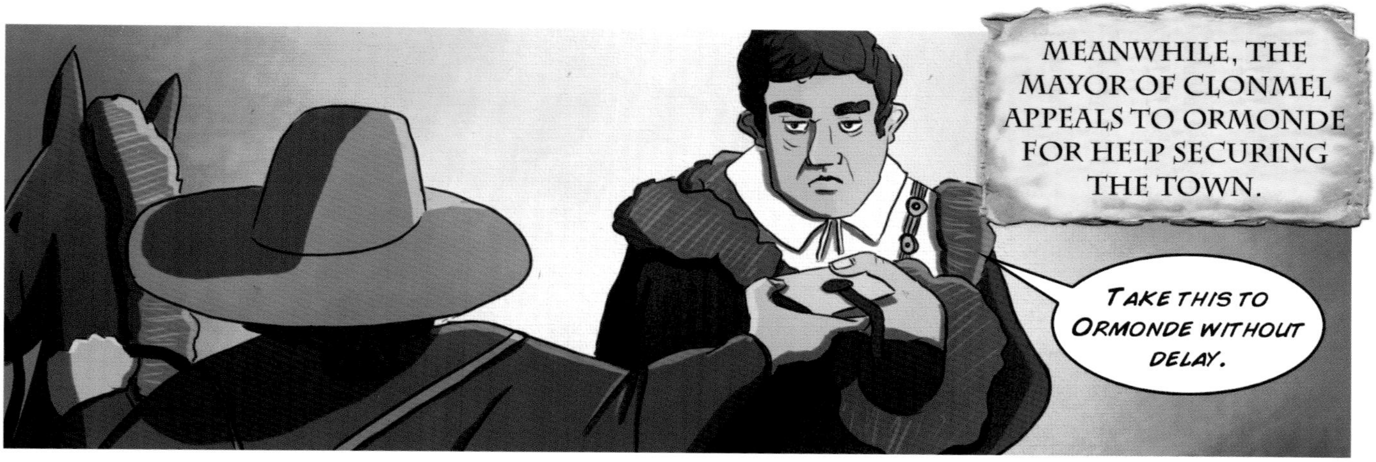
MEANWHILE, THE MAYOR OF CLONMEL APPEALS TO ORMONDE FOR HELP SECURING THE TOWN.
TAKE THIS TO ORMONDE WITHOUT DELAY.

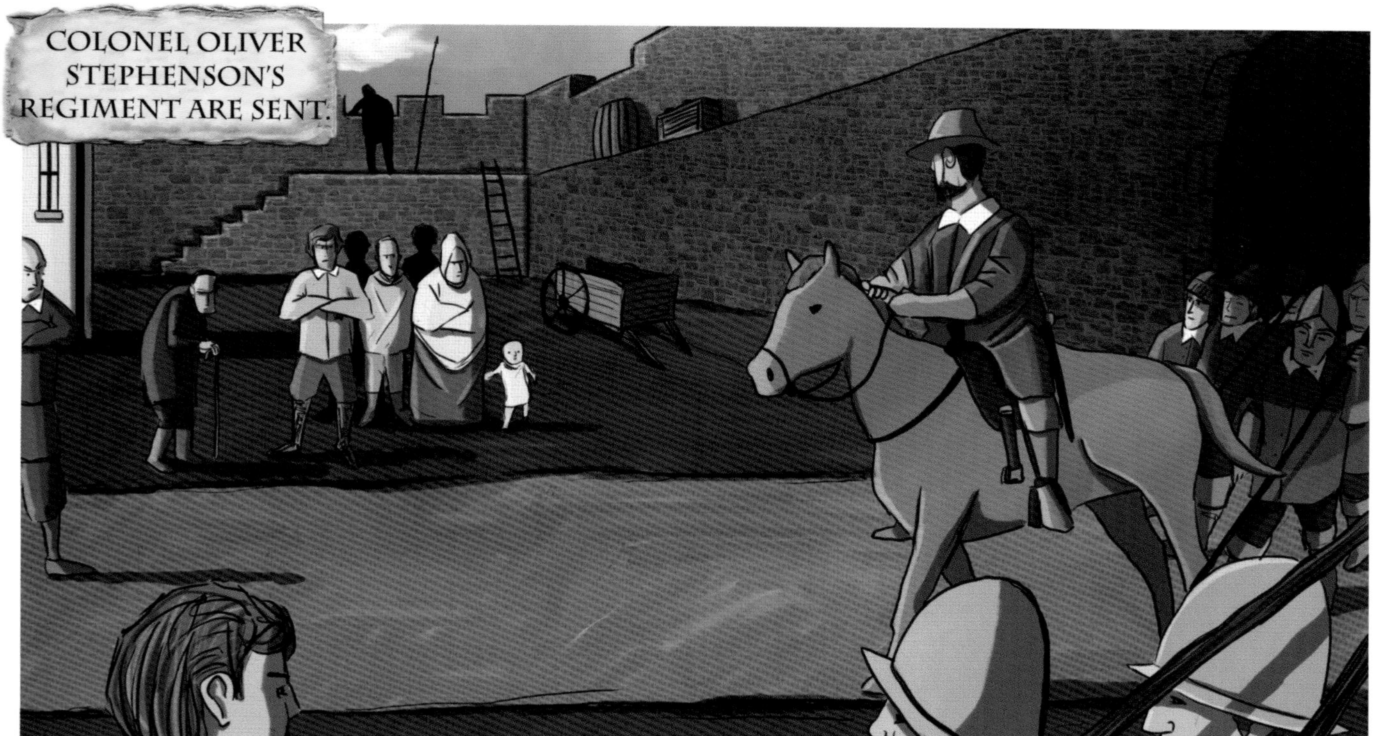
COLONEL OLIVER STEPHENSON'S REGIMENT ARE SENT.

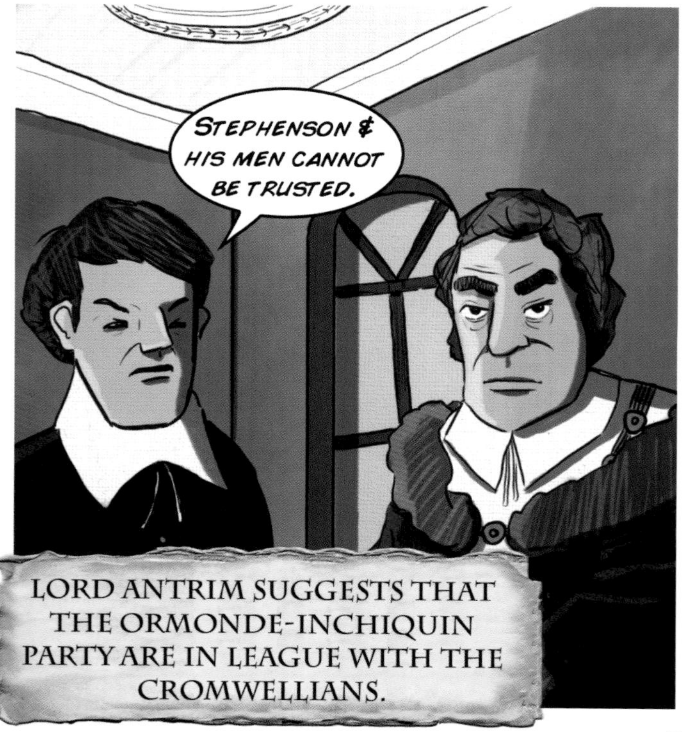
STEPHENSON & HIS MEN CANNOT BE TRUSTED.
LORD ANTRIM SUGGESTS THAT THE ORMONDE-INCHIQUIN PARTY ARE IN LEAGUE WITH THE CROMWELLIANS.

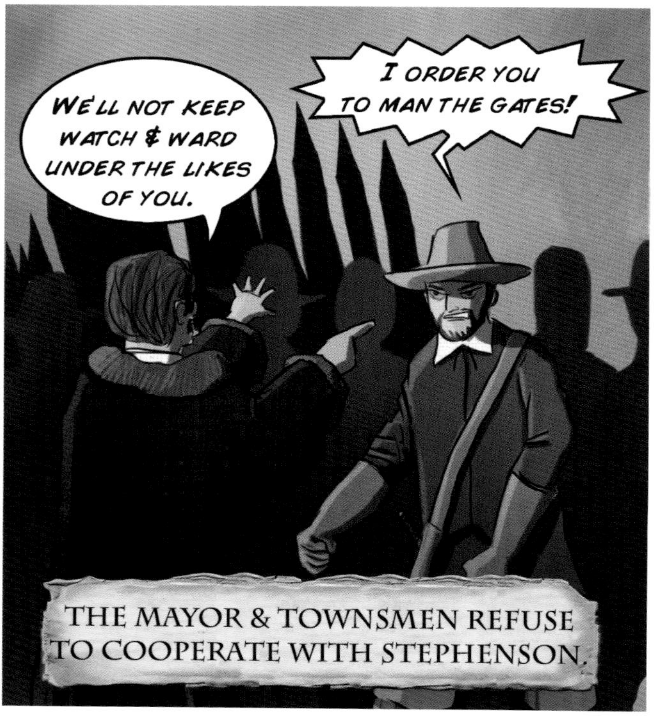
I ORDER YOU TO MAN THE GATES!
WE'LL NOT KEEP WATCH & WARD UNDER THE LIKES OF YOU.
THE MAYOR & TOWNSMEN REFUSE TO COOPERATE WITH STEPHENSON.

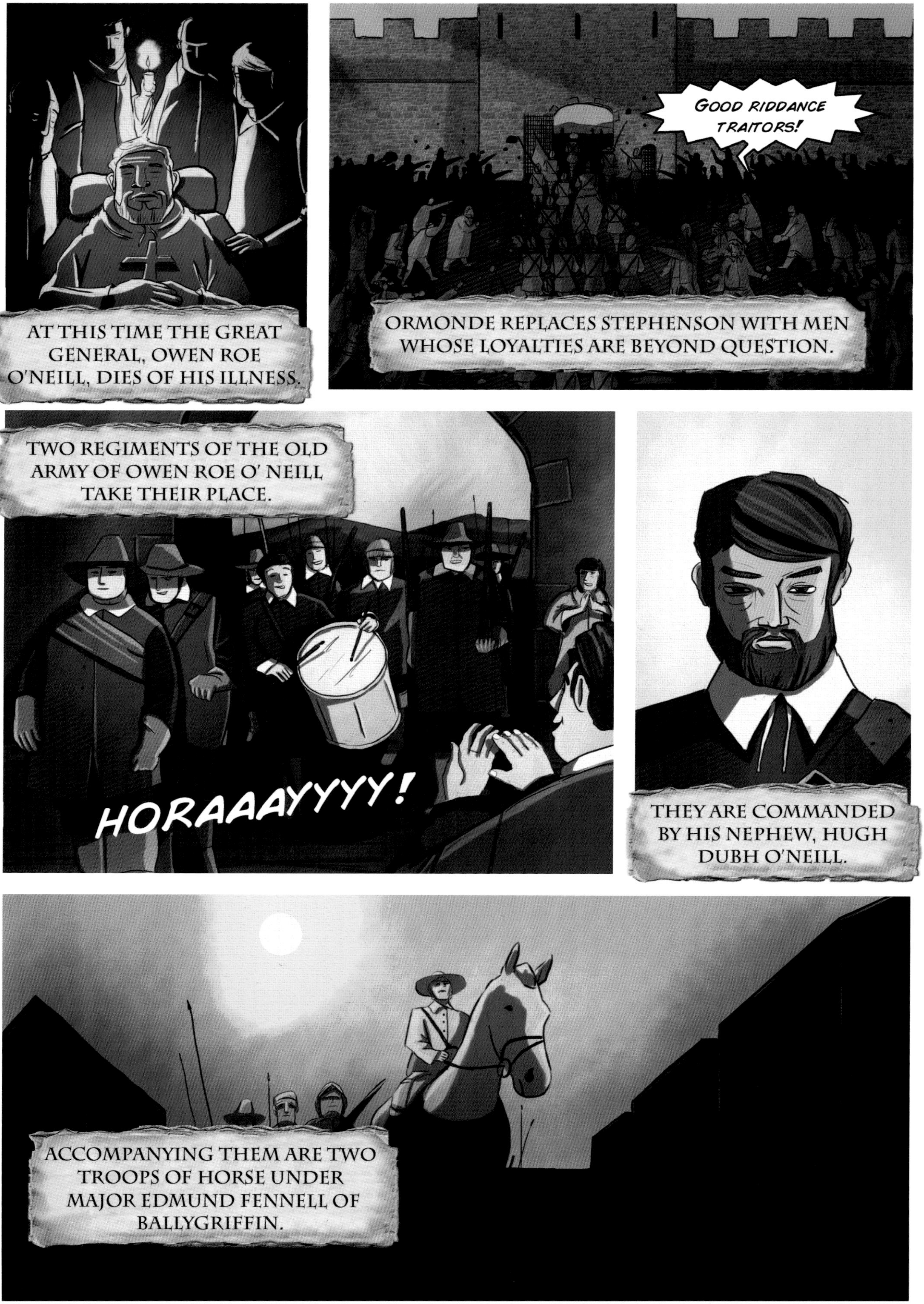
AT THIS TIME THE GREAT GENERAL, OWEN ROE O'NEILL, DIES OF HIS ILLNESS.
GOOD RIDDANCE TRAITORS!
ORMONDE REPLACES STEPHENSON WITH MEN WHOSE LOYALTIES ARE BEYOND QUESTION.
TWO REGIMENTS OF THE OLD ARMY OF OWEN ROE O' NEILL TAKE THEIR PLACE.
HORAAAYYYY!
THEY ARE COMMANDED BY HIS NEPHEW, HUGH DUBH O'NEILL.
ACCOMPANYING THEM ARE TWO TROOPS OF HORSE UNDER MAJOR EDMUND FENNELL OF BALLYGRIFFIN.

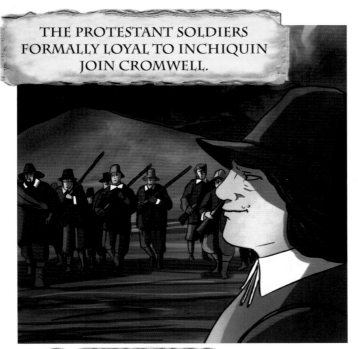

THE PROTESTANT SOLDIERS FORMALLY LOYAL TO INCHIQUIN JOIN CROMWELL.

REINFORCEMENTS ARRIVE FROM ENGLAND.

HE LEAVES HIS WINTER QUARTERS EARLY IN 1650.

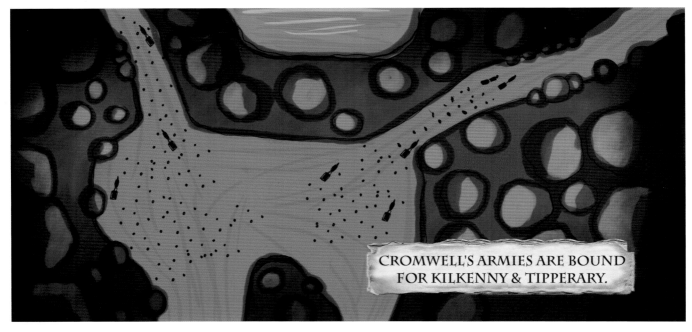

CROMWELL'S ARMIES ARE BOUND FOR KILKENNY & TIPPERARY.

AMID WILD WIND & RAIN CROMWELL REACHES THE GATES OF FETHARD IN TIPPERARY.

SURRENDER THE KEYS TO ME & RECEIVE FAVOURABLE TERMS.

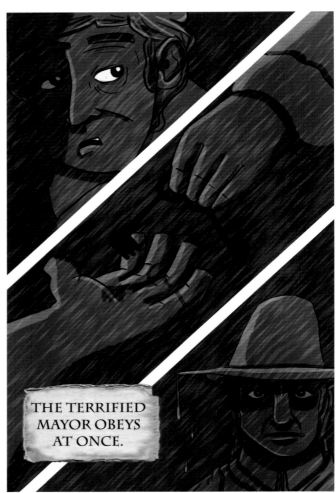

THE TERRIFIED MAYOR OBEYS AT ONCE.

THE NEXT DAY THE PEOPLE OF CASHEL, ALONG WITH THEIR MAYOR, ARRIVE AT FETHARD TO BEG CROMWELL FOR HIS MERCY.

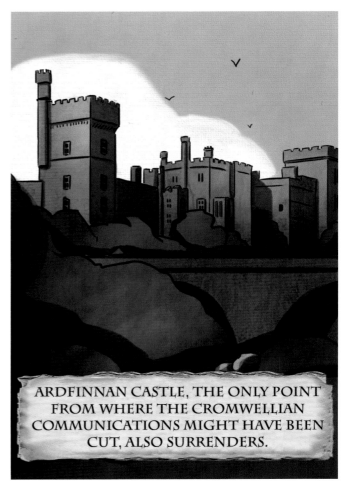

ARDFINNAN CASTLE, THE ONLY POINT FROM WHERE THE CROMWELLIAN COMMUNICATIONS MIGHT HAVE BEEN CUT, ALSO SURRENDERS.

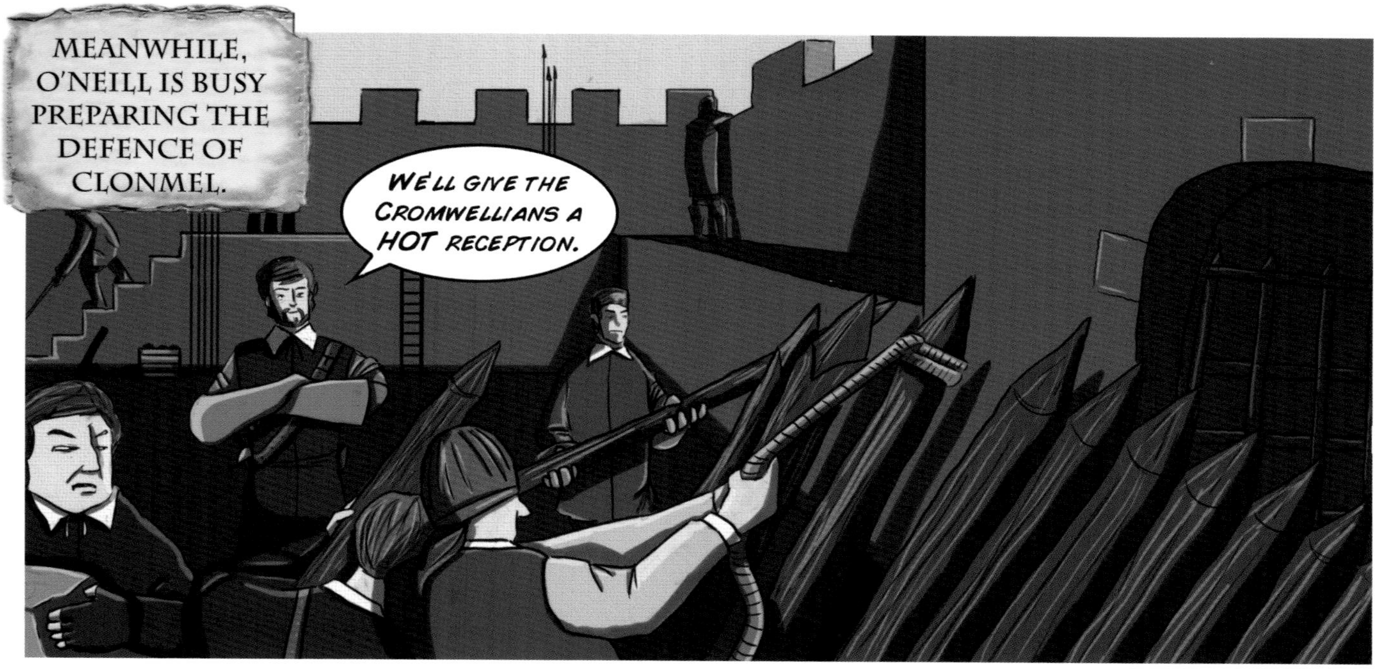
MEANWHILE, O'NEILL IS BUSY PREPARING THE DEFENCE OF CLONMEL.
WE'LL GIVE THE CROMWELLIANS A HOT RECEPTION.

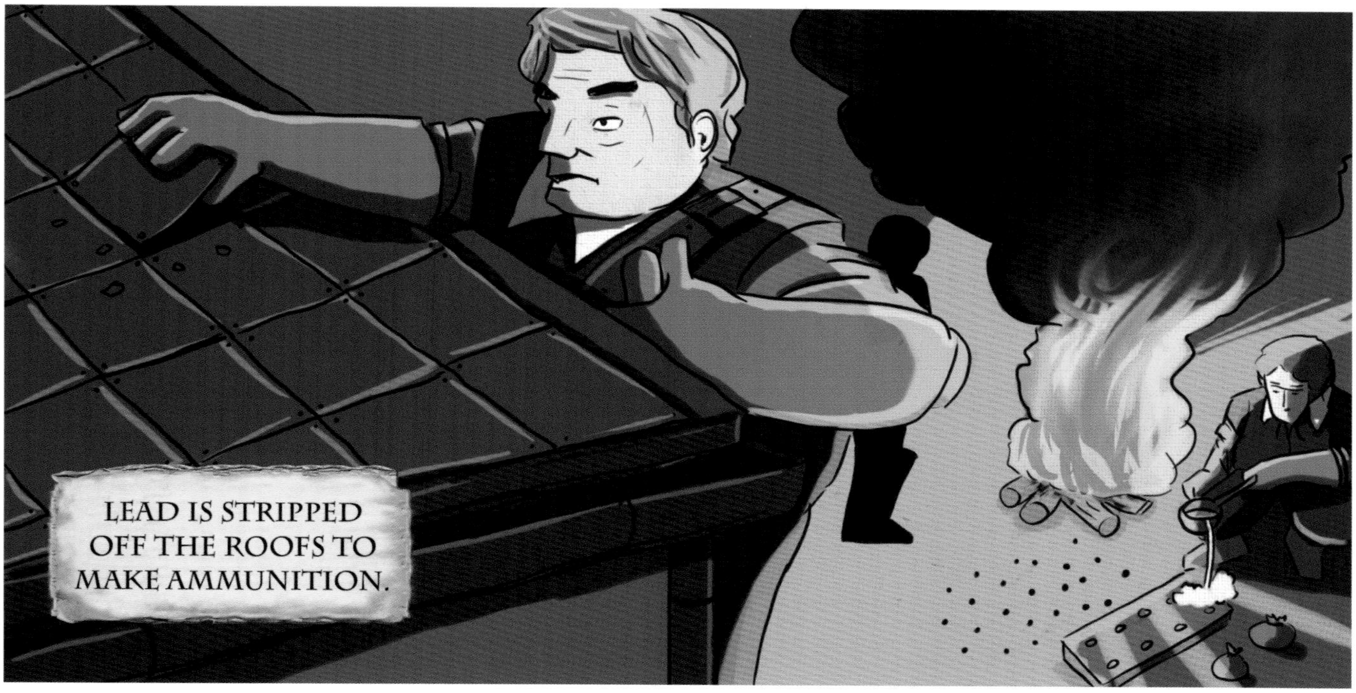
LEAD IS STRIPPED OFF THE ROOFS TO MAKE AMMUNITION.

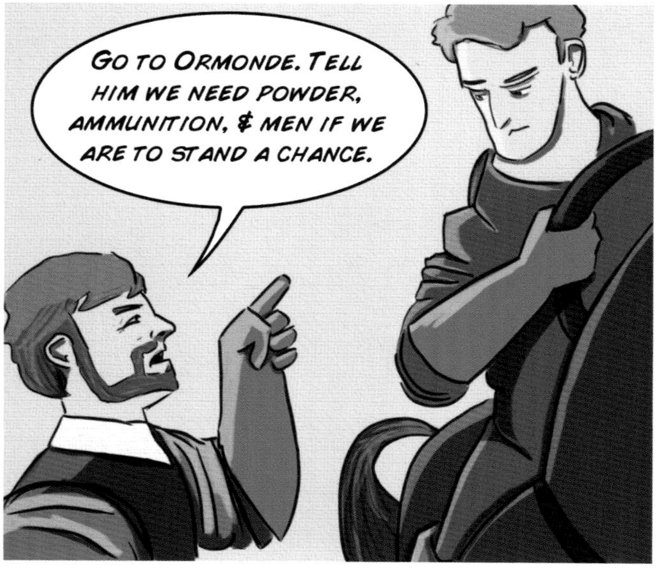
GO TO ORMONDE. TELL HIM WE NEED POWDER, AMMUNITION, & MEN IF WE ARE TO STAND A CHANCE.

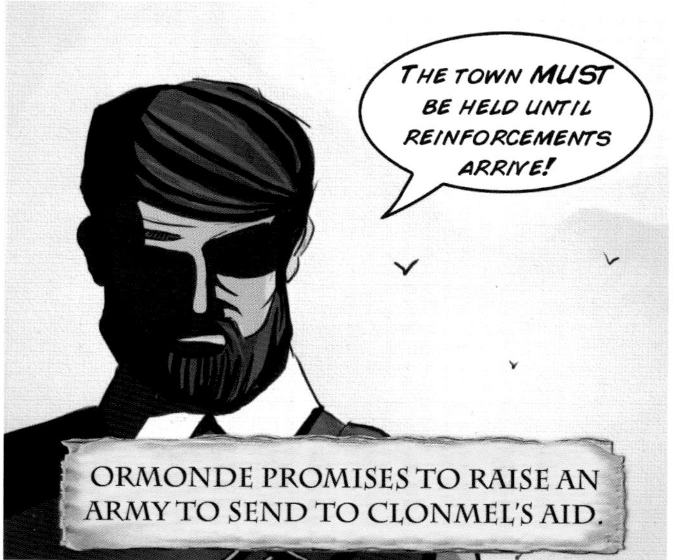
THE TOWN MUST BE HELD UNTIL REINFORCEMENTS ARRIVE!
ORMONDE PROMISES TO RAISE AN ARMY TO SEND TO CLONMEL'S AID.

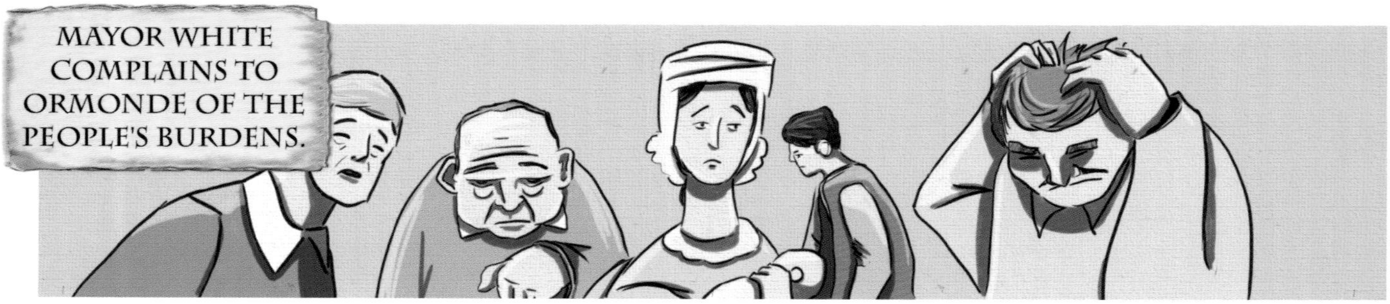
MAYOR WHITE COMPLAINS TO ORMONDE OF THE PEOPLE'S BURDENS.

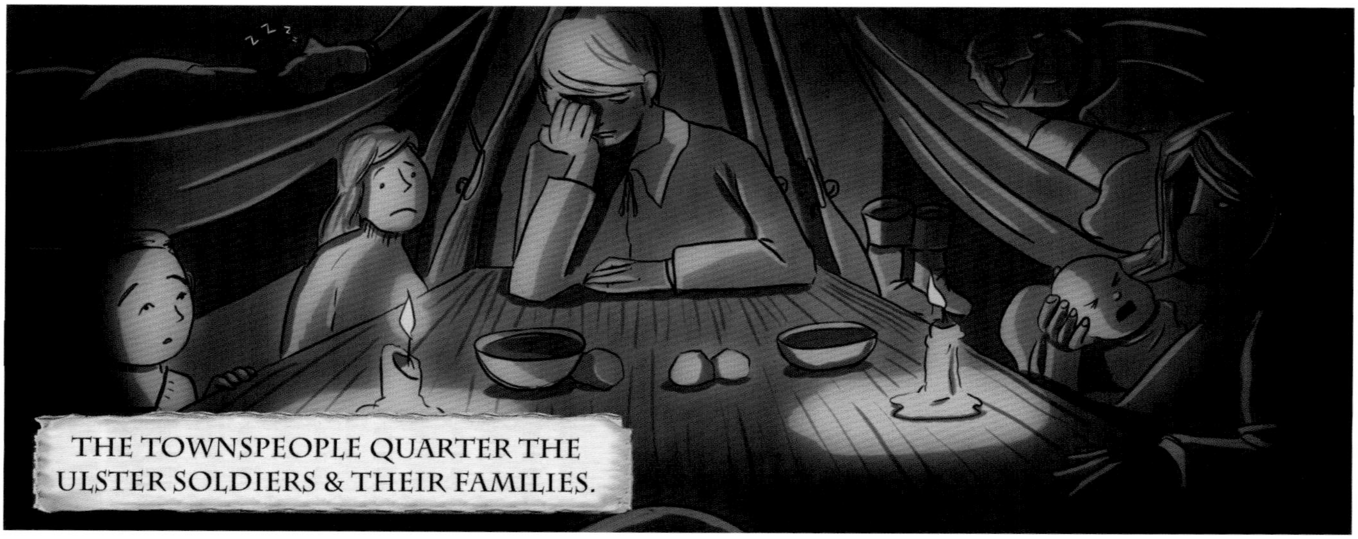
THE TOWNSPEOPLE QUARTER THE ULSTER SOLDIERS & THEIR FAMILIES.

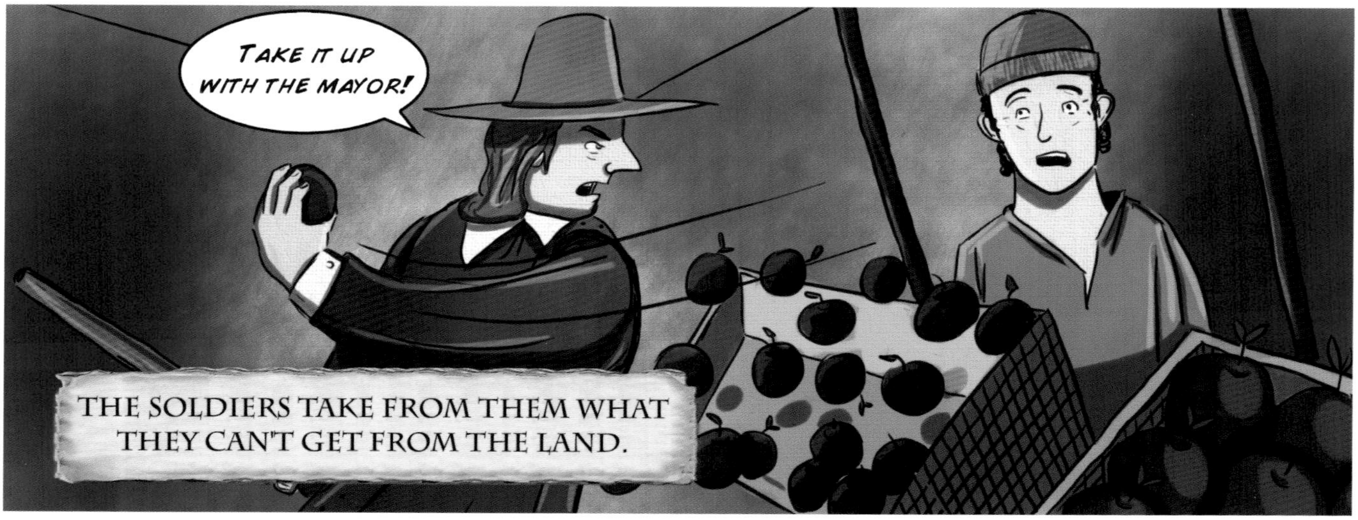
TAKE IT UP WITH THE MAYOR!
THE SOLDIERS TAKE FROM THEM WHAT THEY CAN'T GET FROM THE LAND.

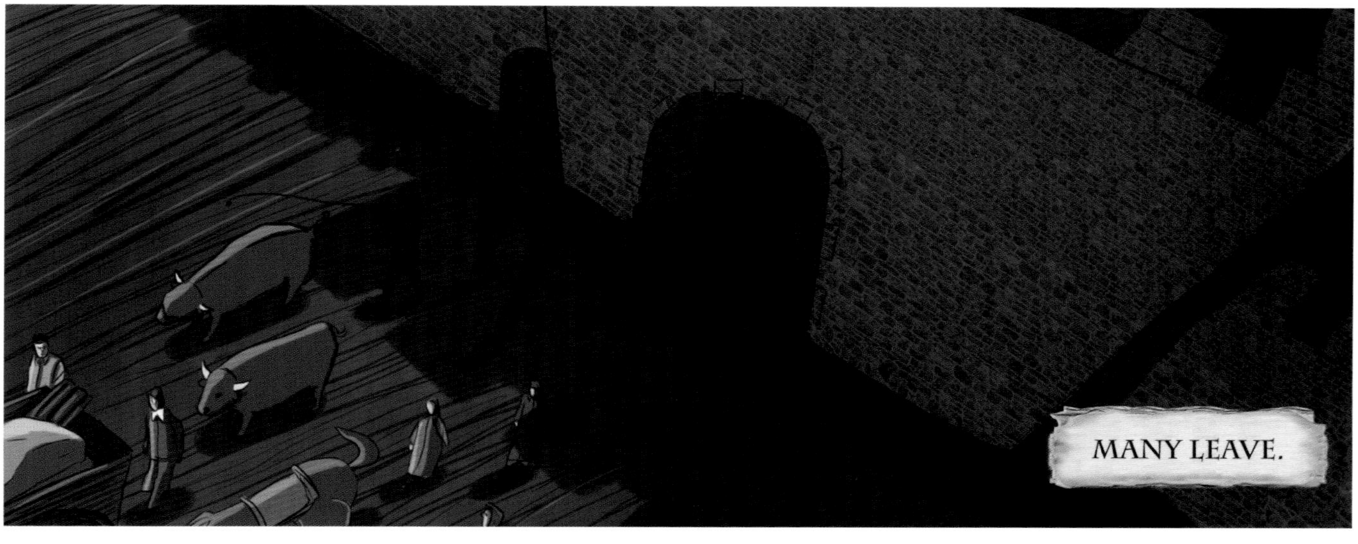
MANY LEAVE.

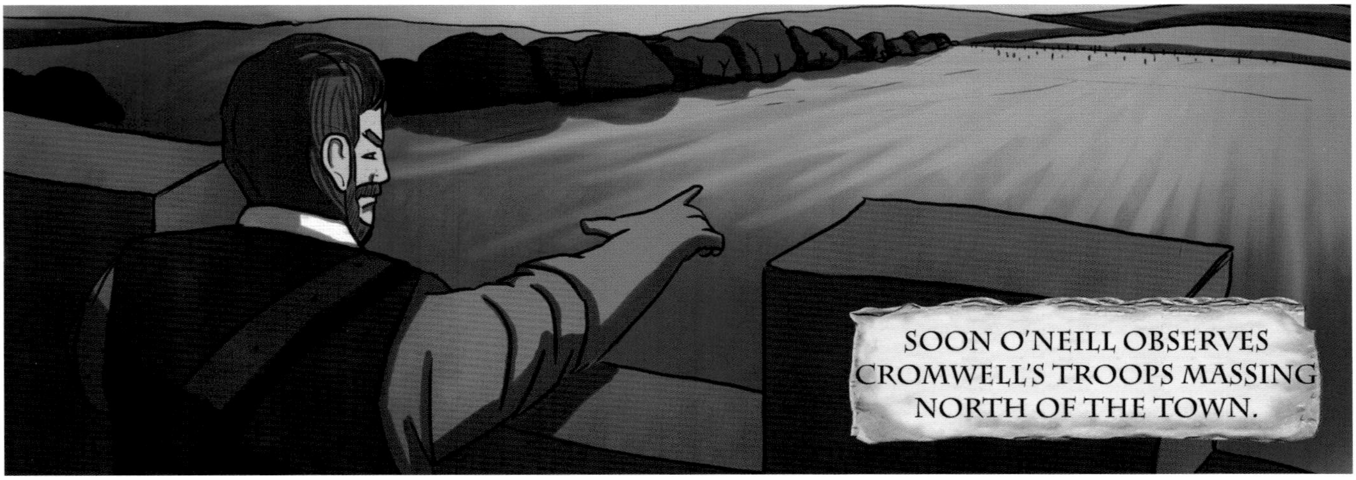
SOON O'NEILL OBSERVES CROMWELL'S TROOPS MASSING NORTH OF THE TOWN.

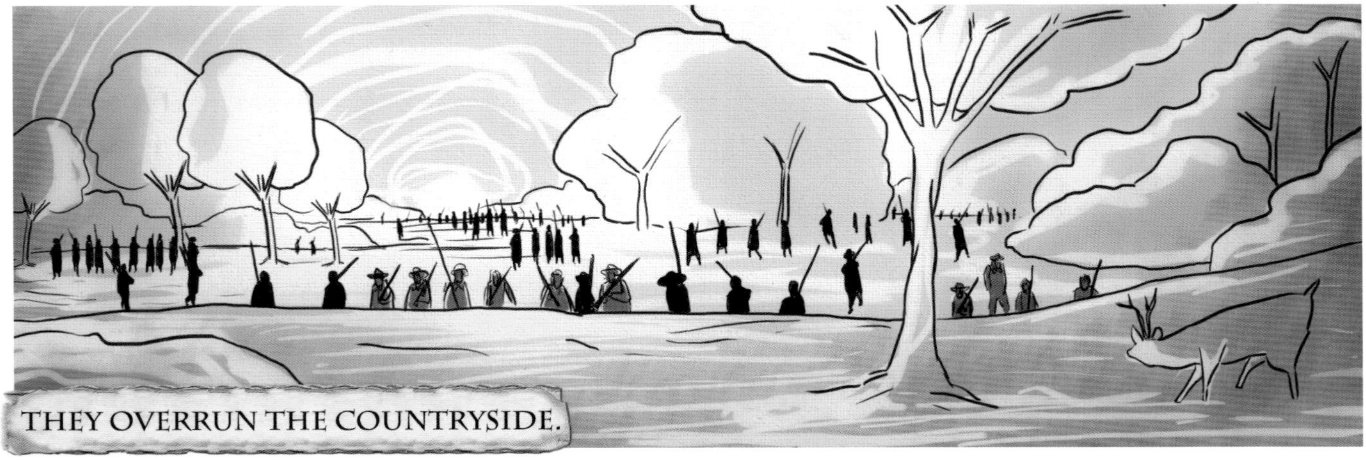
THEY OVERRUN THE COUNTRYSIDE.

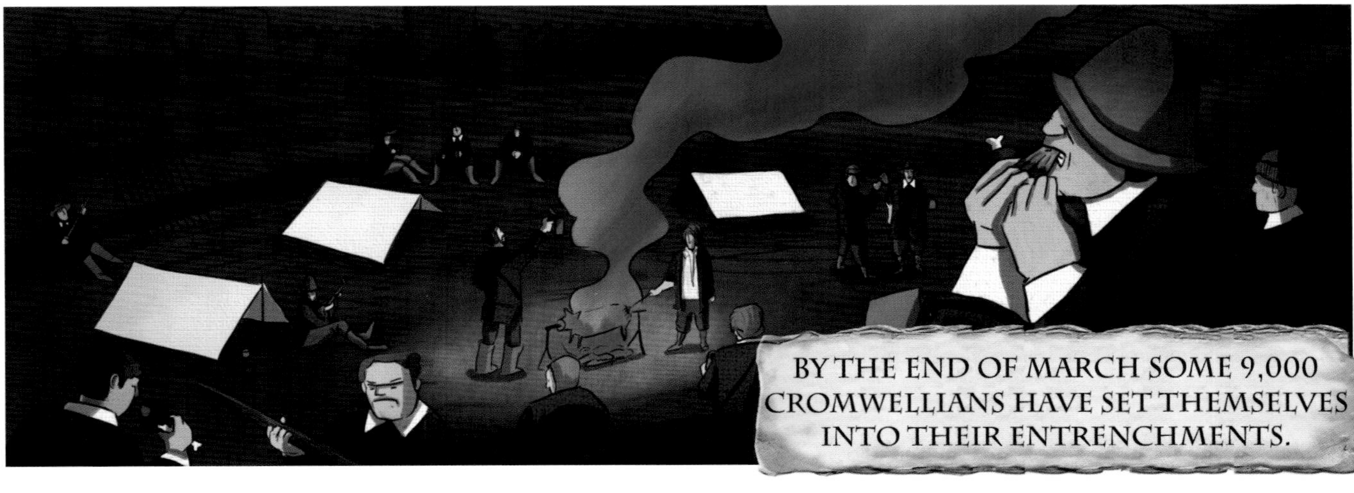
BY THE END OF MARCH SOME 9,000 CROMWELLIANS HAVE SET THEMSELVES INTO THEIR ENTRENCHMENTS.

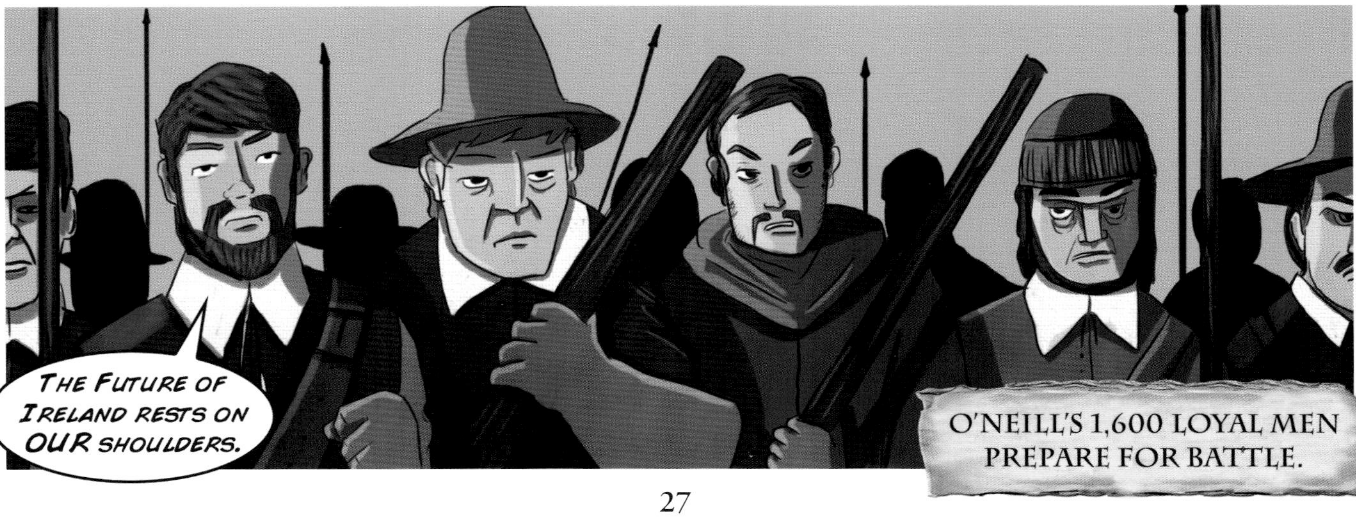
THE FUTURE OF IRELAND RESTS ON OUR SHOULDERS.
O'NEILL'S 1,600 LOYAL MEN PREPARE FOR BATTLE.

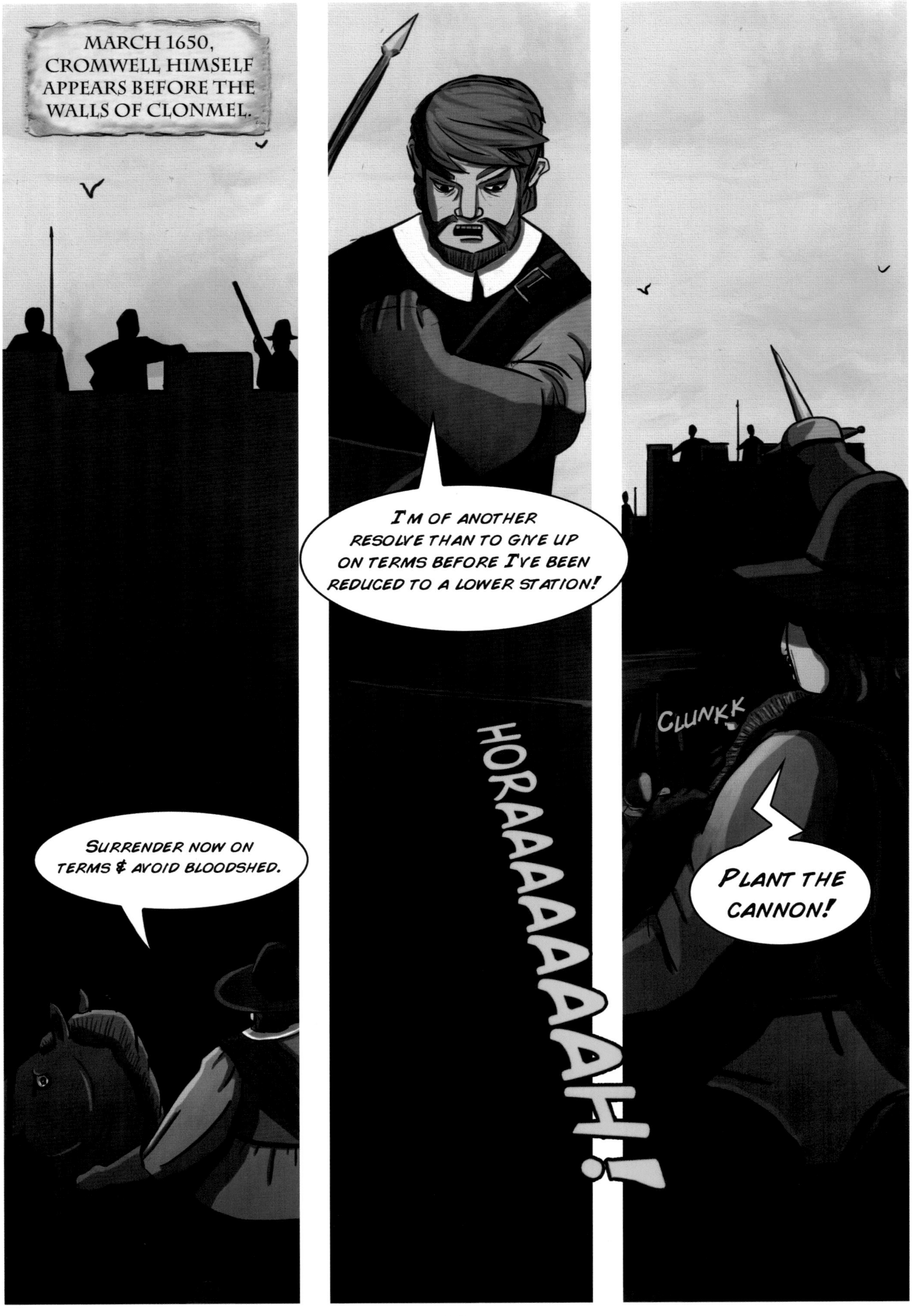
MARCH 1650, CROMWELL HIMSELF APPEARS BEFORE THE WALLS OF CLONMEL.
SURRENDER NOW ON TERMS & AVOID BLOODSHED.
I'M OF ANOTHER RESOLVE THAN TO GIVE UP ON TERMS BEFORE I'VE BEEN REDUCED TO A LOWER STATION!
HORAAAAAAAH!
CLUNKK
PLANT THE CANNON!

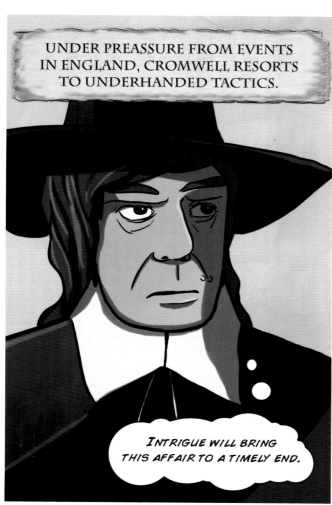

UNDER PREASSURE FROM EVENTS IN ENGLAND, CROMWELL RESORTS TO UNDERHANDED TACTICS.

INTRIGUE WILL BRING THIS AFFAIR TO A TIMELY END.

FENNELL I PRESUME?

YES MY LORD

HE SUMMONS MAJOR FENNELL TO HIS TENT.

IF YOU WERE TO GARRISON THE NORTH GATE WITH YOUR MEN & ALLOW SOME OF MY TROOPS TO ENTER AT MIDNIGHT TOMORROW, A PARDON AND £500 WOULD BE YOURS.

CLINKK

AGREED.

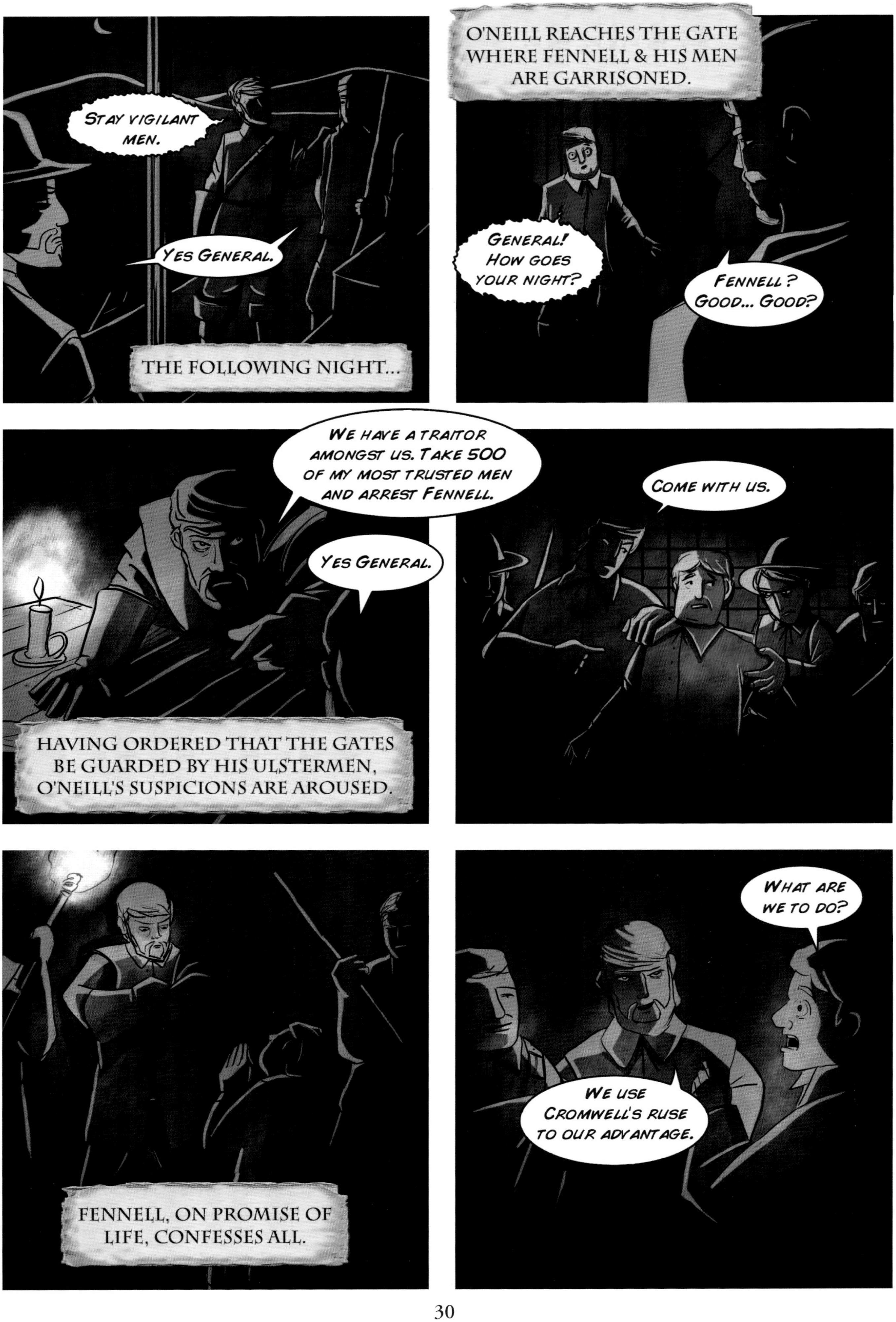
STAY VIGILANT MEN.
YES GENERAL.
THE FOLLOWING NIGHT...
O'NEILL REACHES THE GATE WHERE FENNELL & HIS MEN ARE GARRISONED.
GENERAL! HOW GOES YOUR NIGHT?
FENNELL? GOOD... GOOD?
WE HAVE A TRAITOR AMONGST US. TAKE 500 OF MY MOST TRUSTED MEN AND ARREST FENNELL.
YES GENERAL.
HAVING ORDERED THAT THE GATES BE GUARDED BY HIS ULSTERMEN, O'NEILL'S SUSPICIONS ARE AROUSED.
COME WITH US.
FENNELL, ON PROMISE OF LIFE, CONFESSES ALL.
WHAT ARE WE TO DO?
WE USE CROMWELL'S RUSE TO OUR ADVANTAGE.

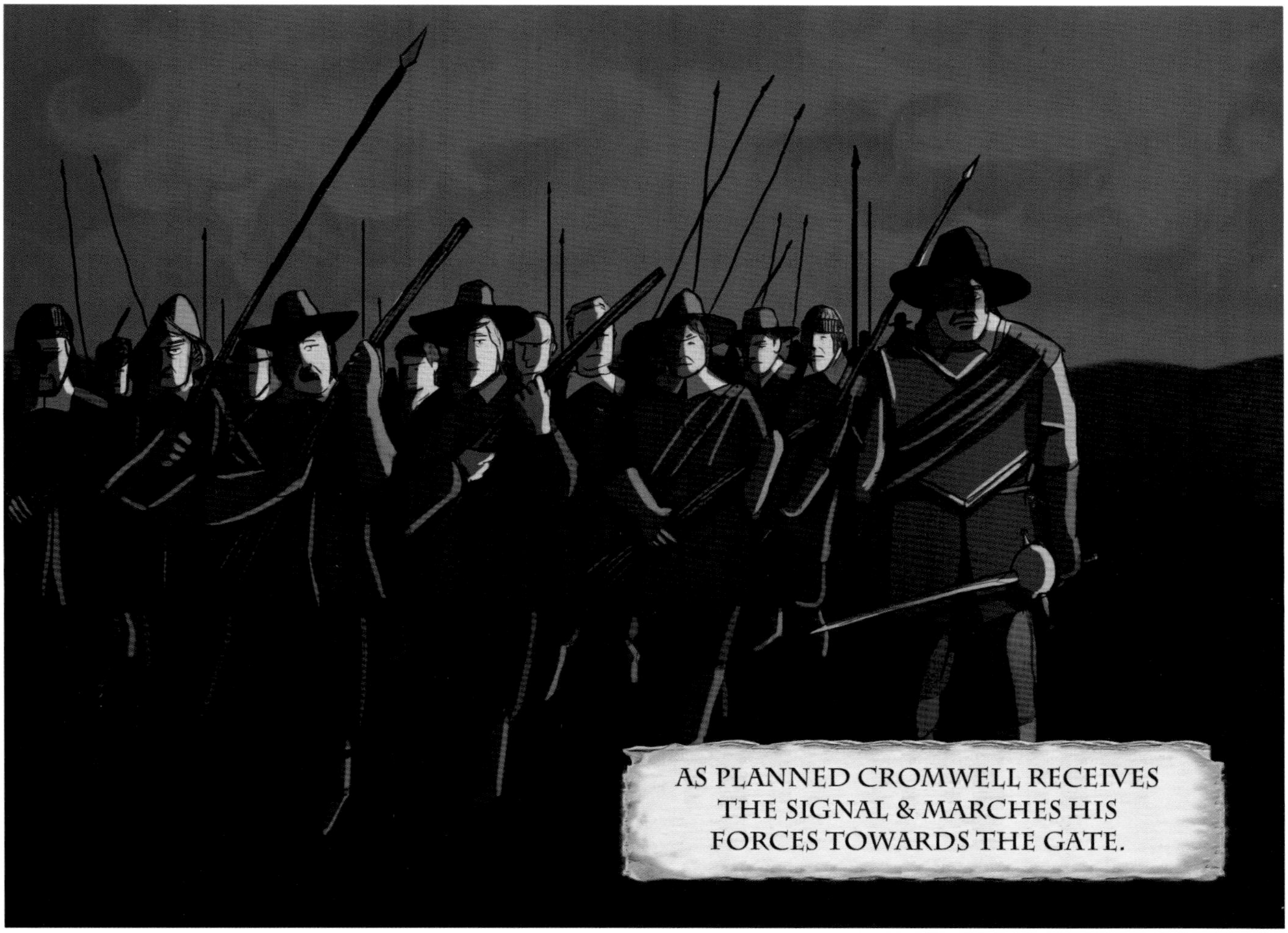
AS PLANNED CROMWELL RECEIVES THE SIGNAL & MARCHES HIS FORCES TOWARDS THE GATE.

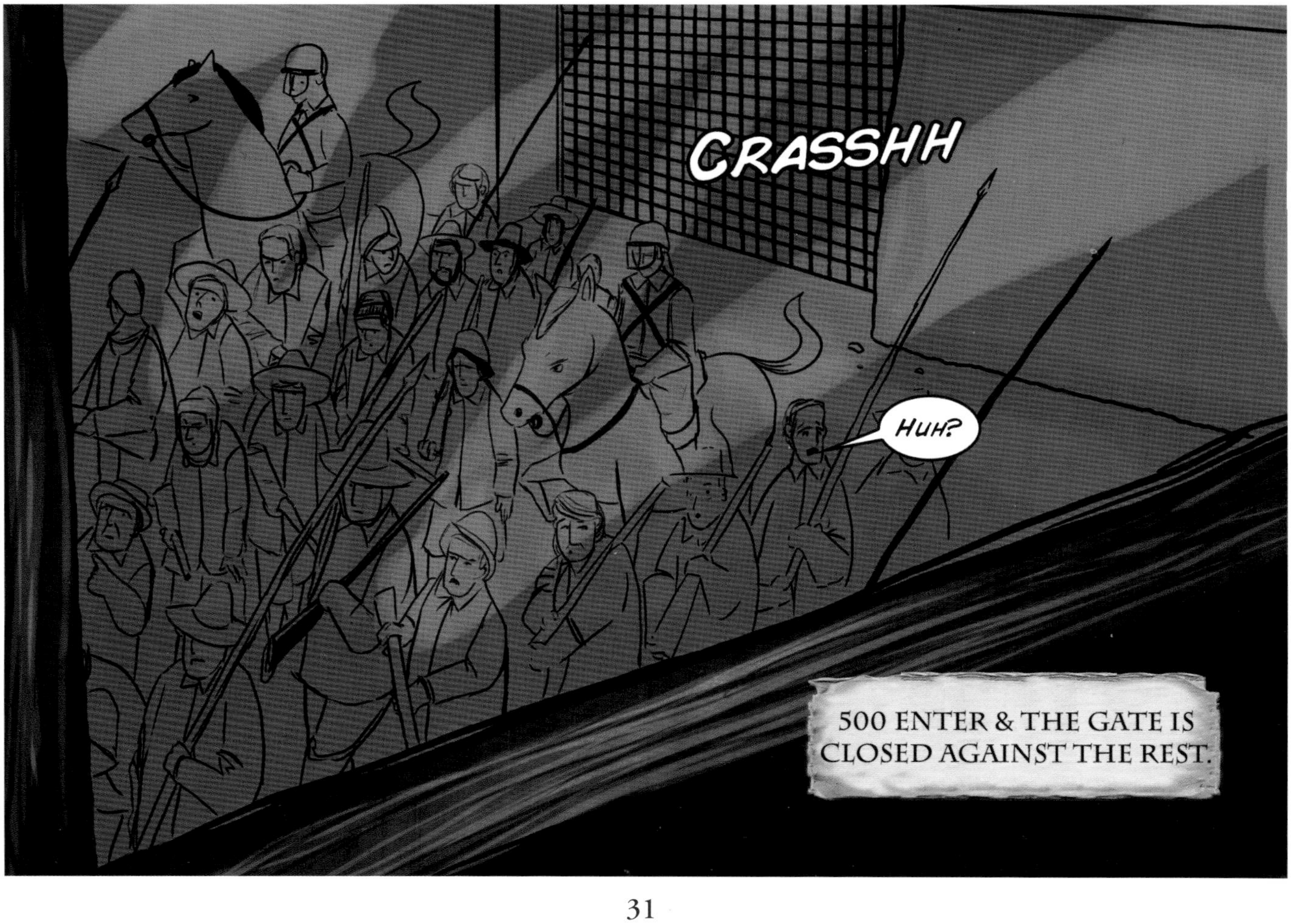
CRASSHH
HUH?
500 ENTER & THE GATE IS CLOSED AGAINST THE REST.

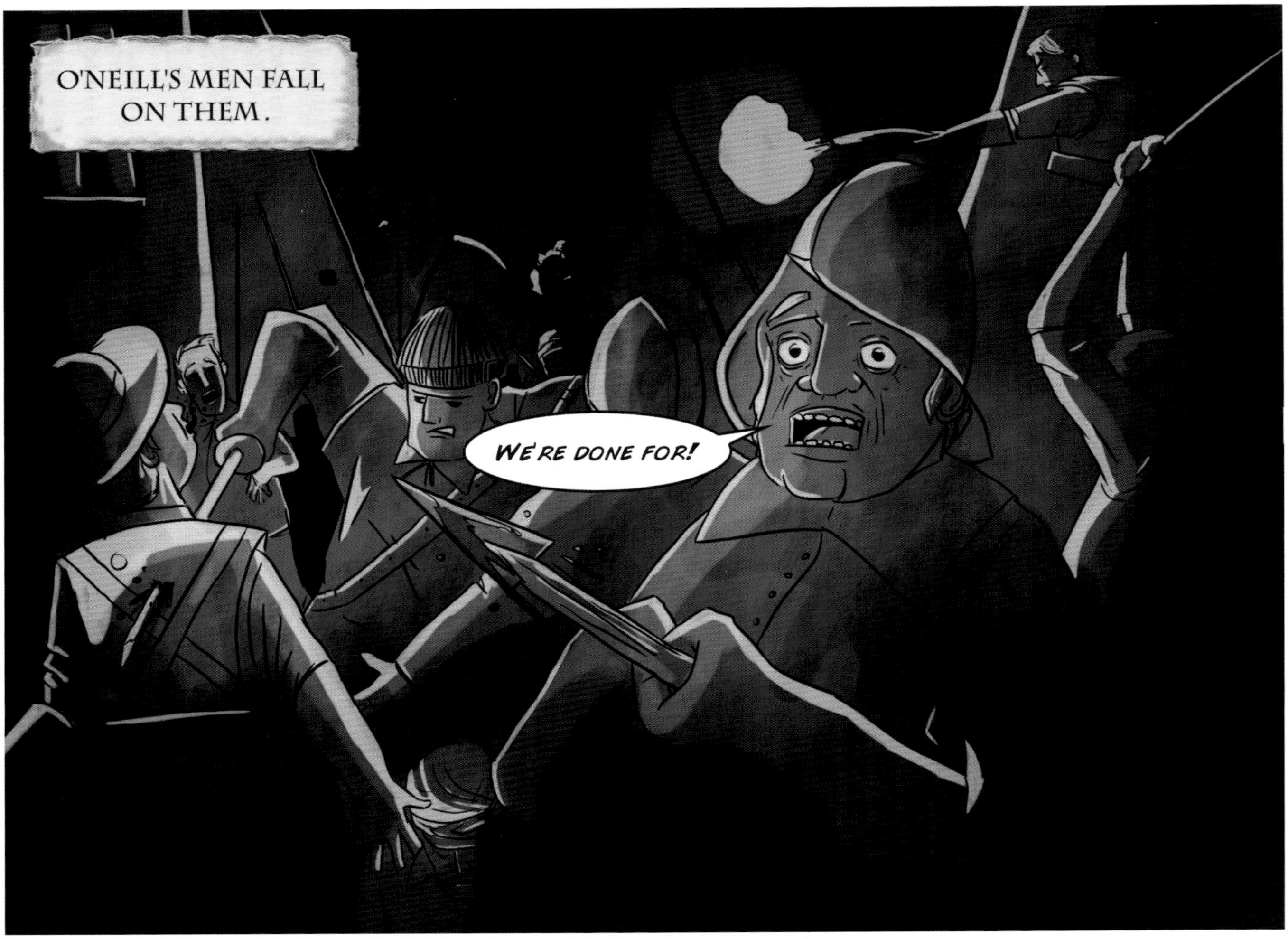
O'NEILL'S MEN FALL ON THEM.
WE'RE DONE FOR!

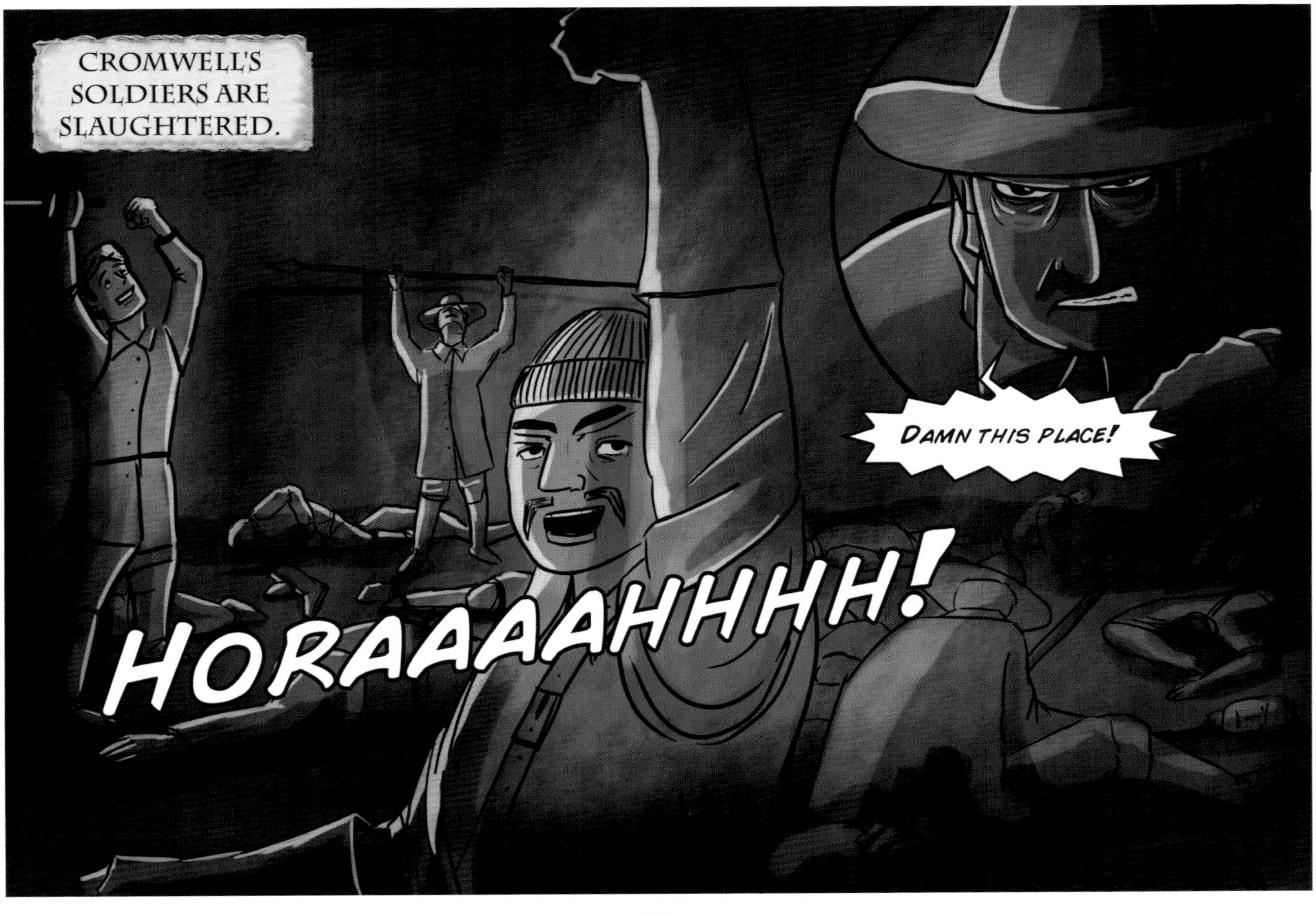
CROMWELL'S SOLDIERS ARE SLAUGHTERED.
DAMN THIS PLACE!
HORAAAAHHHH!

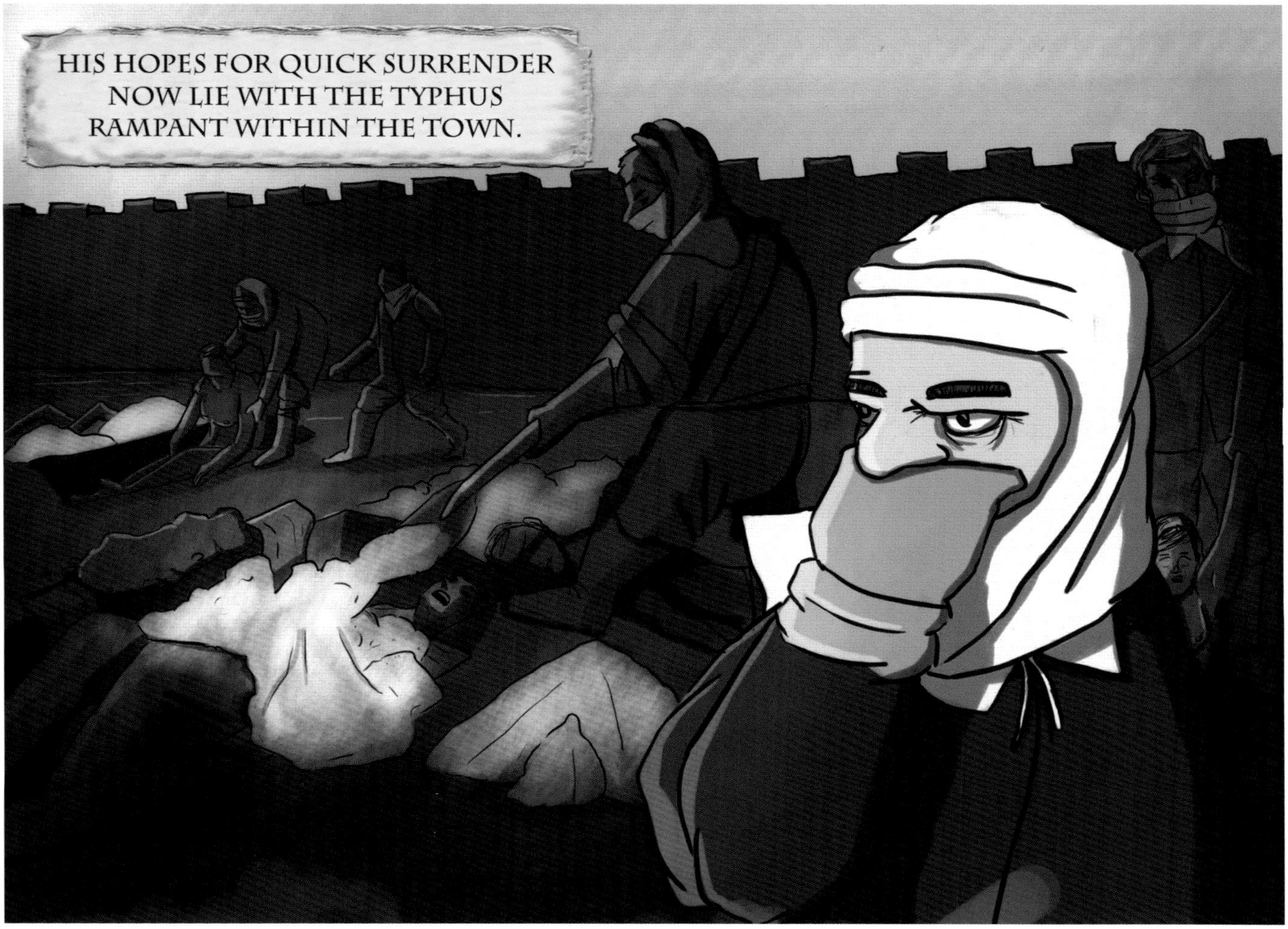
HIS HOPES FOR QUICK SURRENDER NOW LIE WITH THE TYPHUS RAMPANT WITHIN THE TOWN.

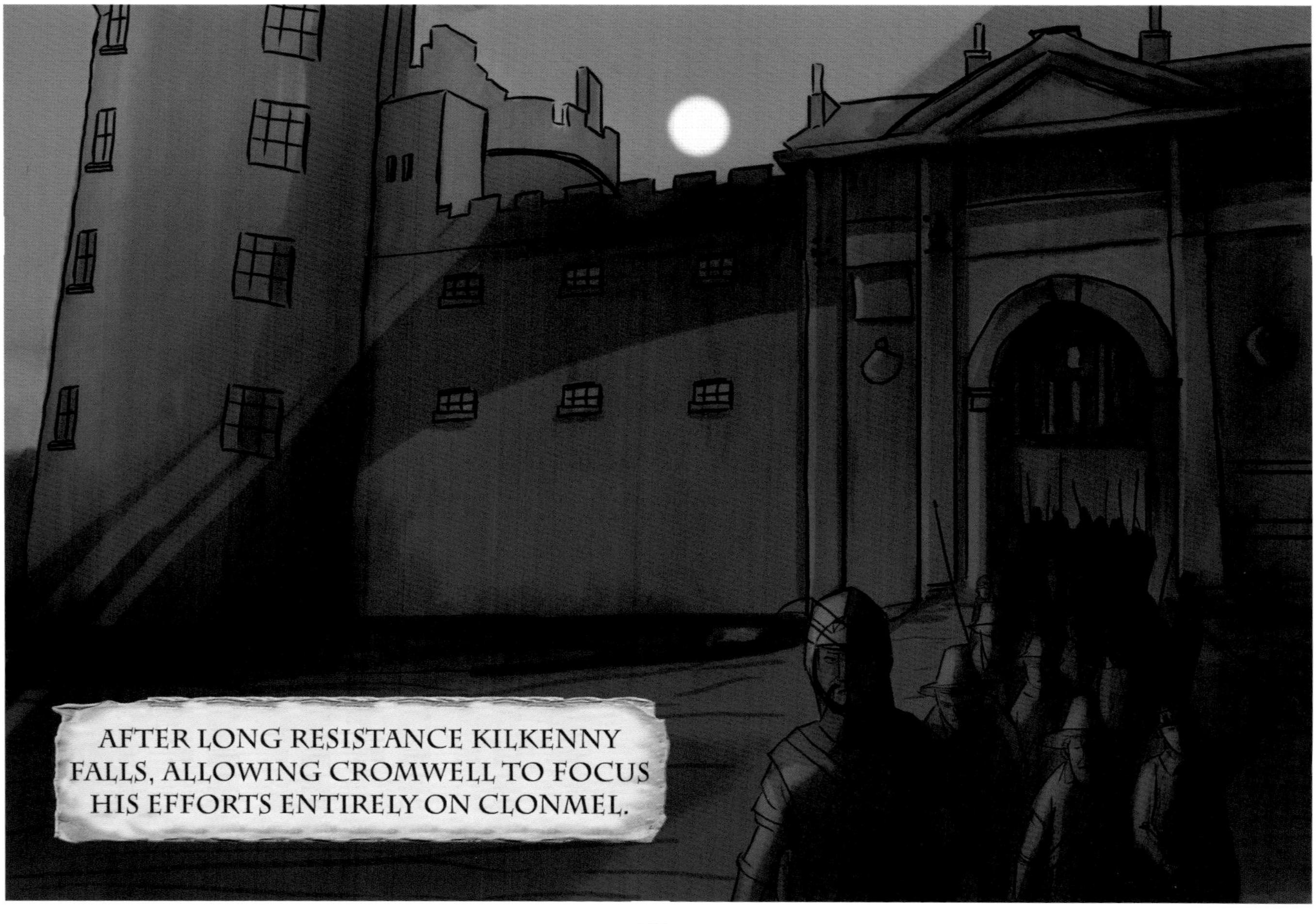
AFTER LONG RESISTANCE KILKENNY FALLS, ALLOWING CROMWELL TO FOCUS HIS EFFORTS ENTIRELY ON CLONMEL.

ORMONDE FAILS TO RAISE AN ARMY. HOWEVER, LORD ROCHE ASSEMBLES A LARGE FORCE IN CORK.

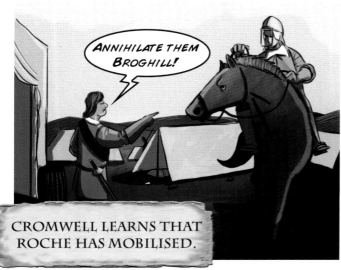

ANNIHILATE THEM BROGHILL!

CROMWELL LEARNS THAT ROCHE HAS MOBILISED.

MANOEUVRE THE TROOPS TO MACROOM!

ROCHE SUSPECTS HE HAS BEEN DISCOVERED.

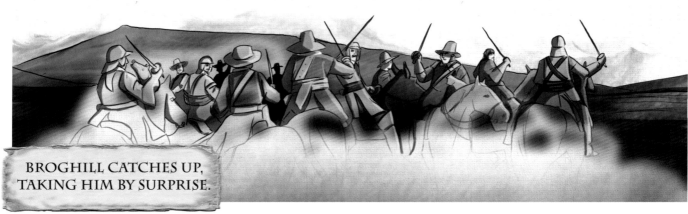

BROGHILL CATCHES UP, TAKING HIM BY SURPRISE.

ROCHE'S DEFEATED ARMY ESCAPE INTO THE HILLS & BOGS OF KERRY, WHERE THE ENGLISH CAN'T FOLLOW.

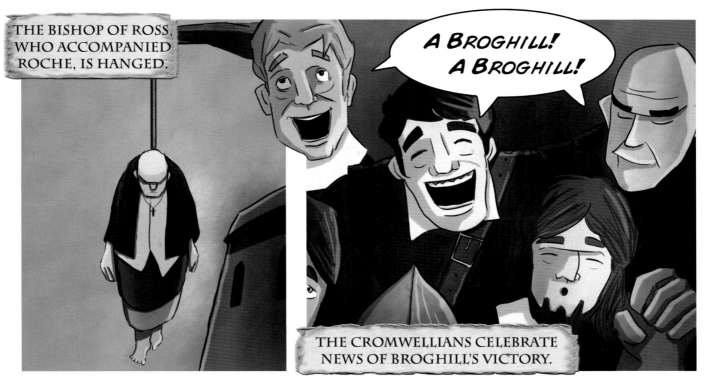

THE BISHOP OF ROSS, WHO ACCOMPANIED ROCHE, IS HANGED.

A BROGHILL! A BROGHILL!

THE CROMWELLIANS CELEBRATE NEWS OF BROGHILL'S VICTORY.

THE PARISH PRIEST OF ARDFINNAN IS BROUGHT BEFORE THE WALLS OF CLONMEL.

WHERE HE IS EXECUTED.

WE'LL SELL OUR LIVES DEARLY!

O'NEILL PRESERVES MORALE.

CROMWELL'S CANNONS BEGIN TO SPEAK AGAINST THE NORTH WALL.

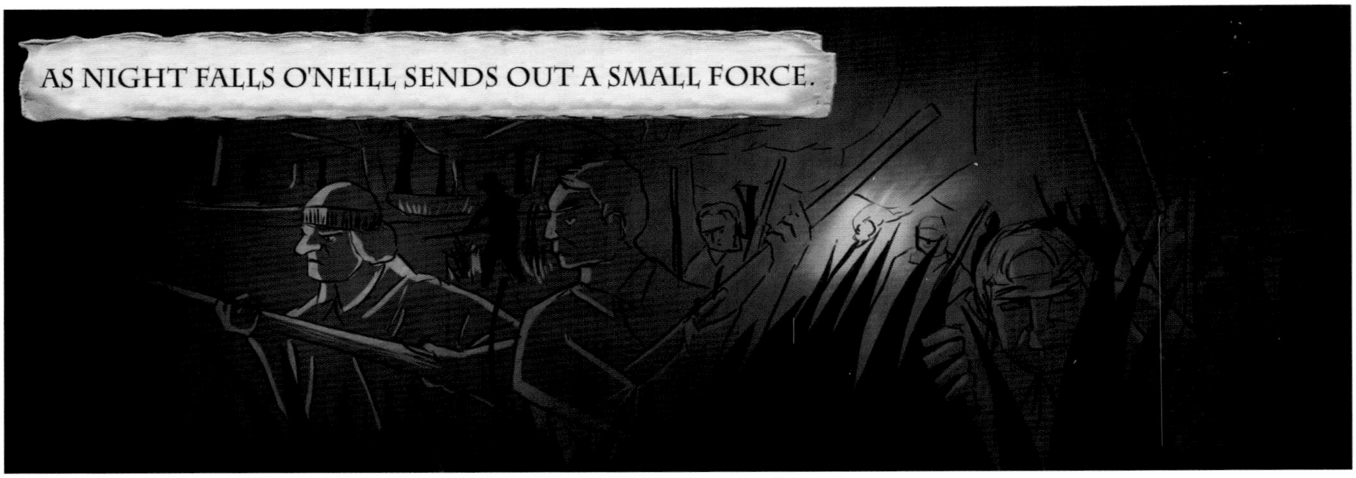
AS NIGHT FALLS O'NEILL SENDS OUT A SMALL FORCE.

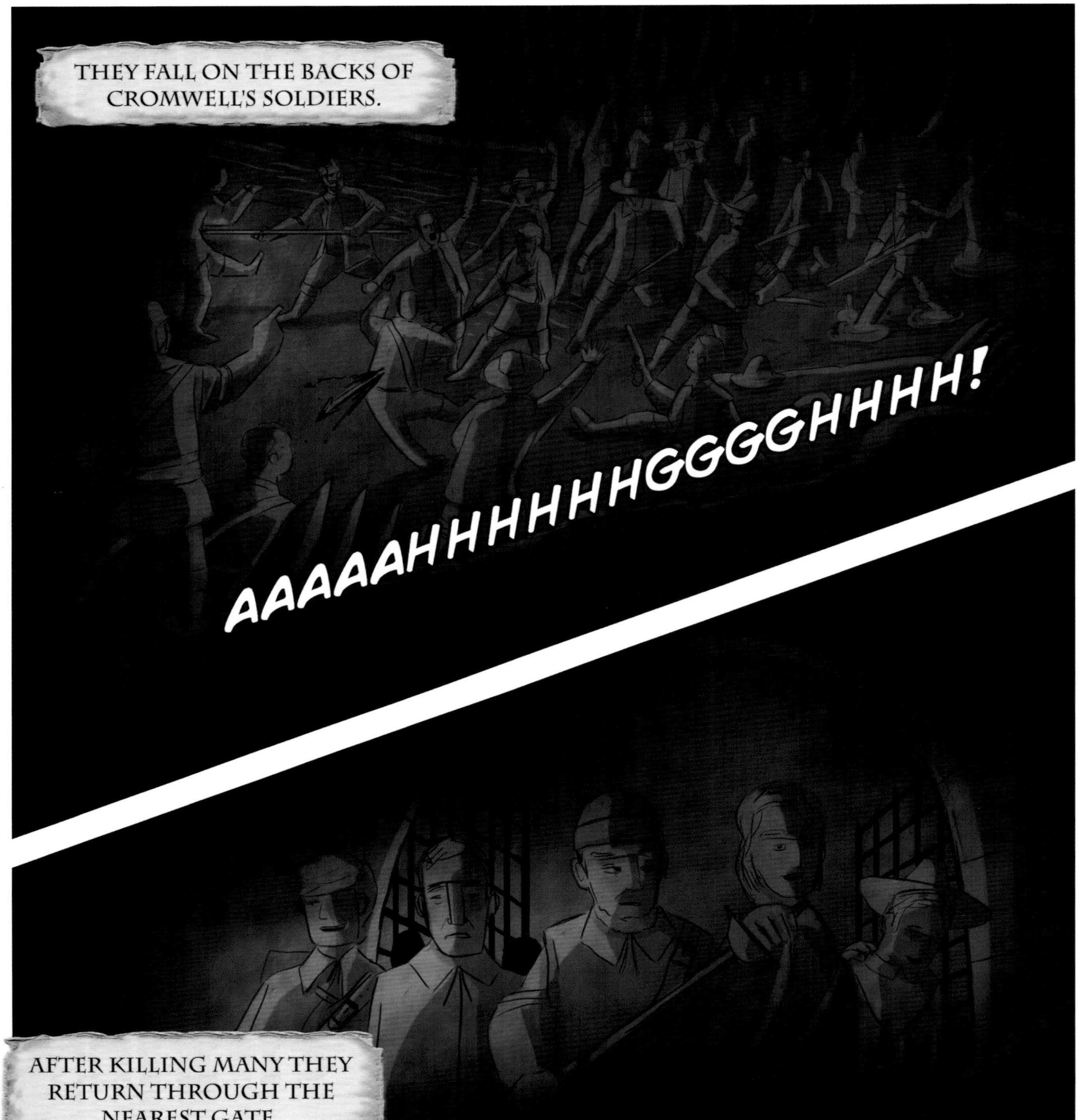
THEY FALL ON THE BACKS OF CROMWELL'S SOLDIERS.
AAAAAHHHHHHGGGGHHHHH!
AFTER KILLING MANY THEY RETURN THROUGH THE NEAREST GATE.

BY MAY THE WALL IS FALLING.

O'NEILL PUTS THE POPULATION OF CLONMEL TO WORK.

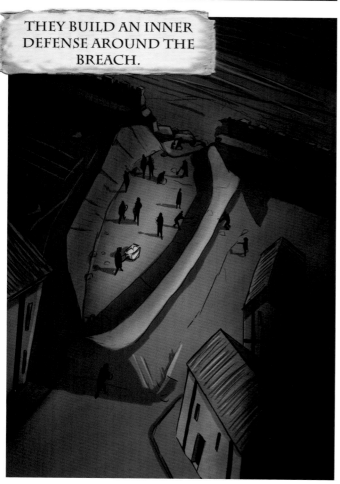

THEY BUILD AN INNER DEFENSE AROUND THE BREACH.

MUSKETMEN LINE THE WALLS. CANNONS LOADED WITH CHAINSHOT SEAL THE END.

NEXT MORNING CROMWELL OPENS THE BREACH.

HE PLANS FOR THE INFANTRY TO STORM THE BREACH & OPEN THE NORTH GATE FOR HIS CAVALRY.

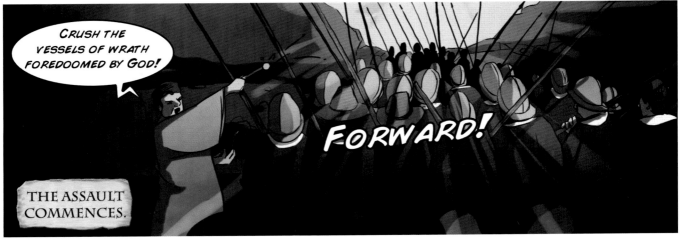

CRUSH THE VESSELS OF WRATH FOREDOOMED BY GOD!

FORWARD!

THE ASSAULT COMMENCES.

THEY PILE IN UNTILL NO MORE CAN ENTER.

FIRE!

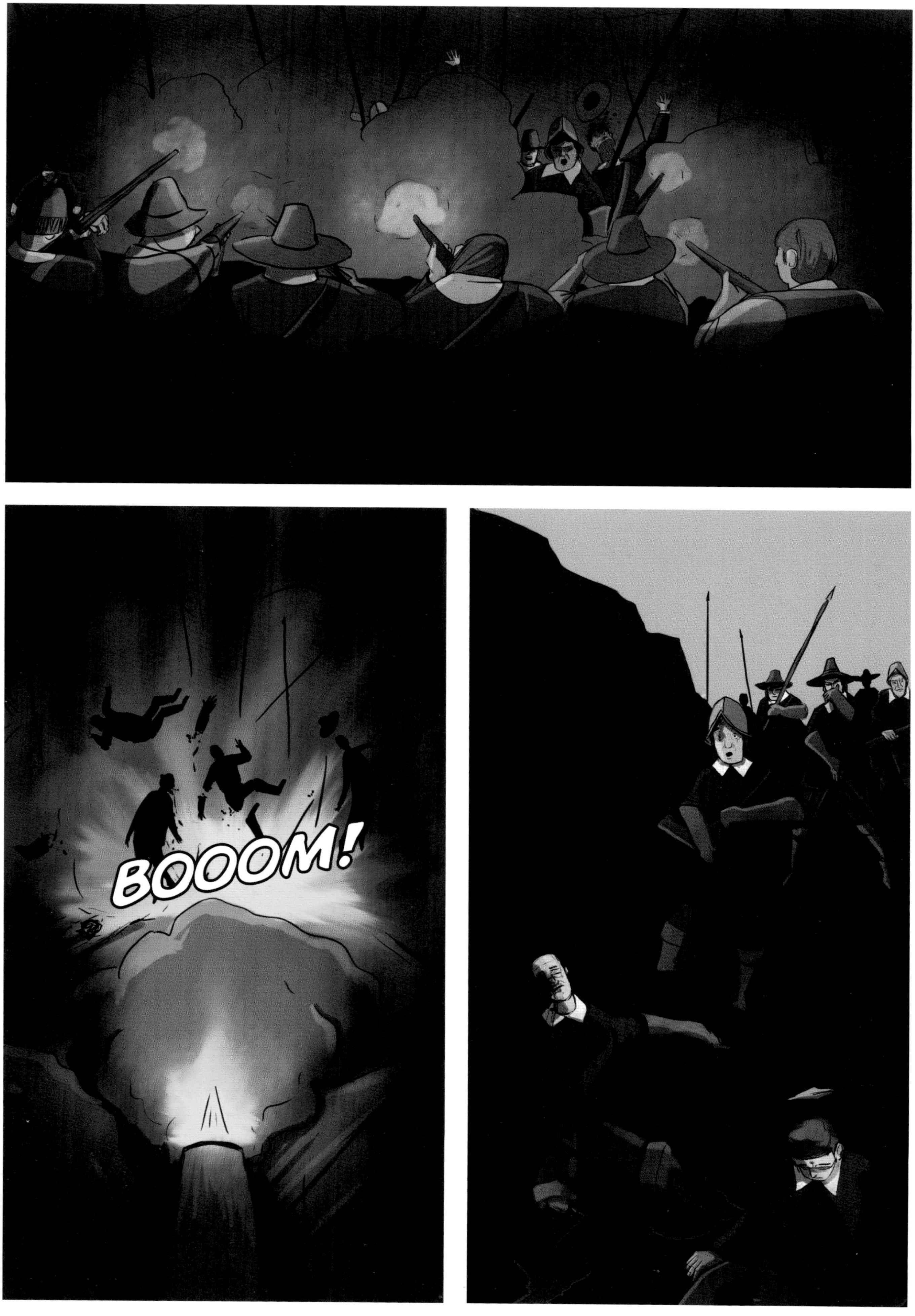
BOOOM!

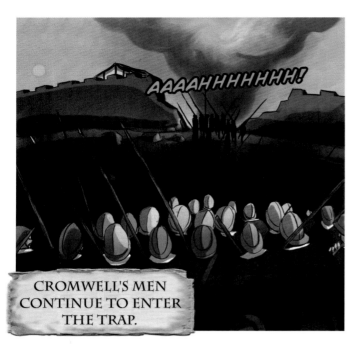

AAAAHHHHHHH!

CROMWELL'S MEN CONTINUE TO ENTER THE TRAP.

THE ULSTER PIKEMEN RUSH IN TO JOIN THE FIGHT.

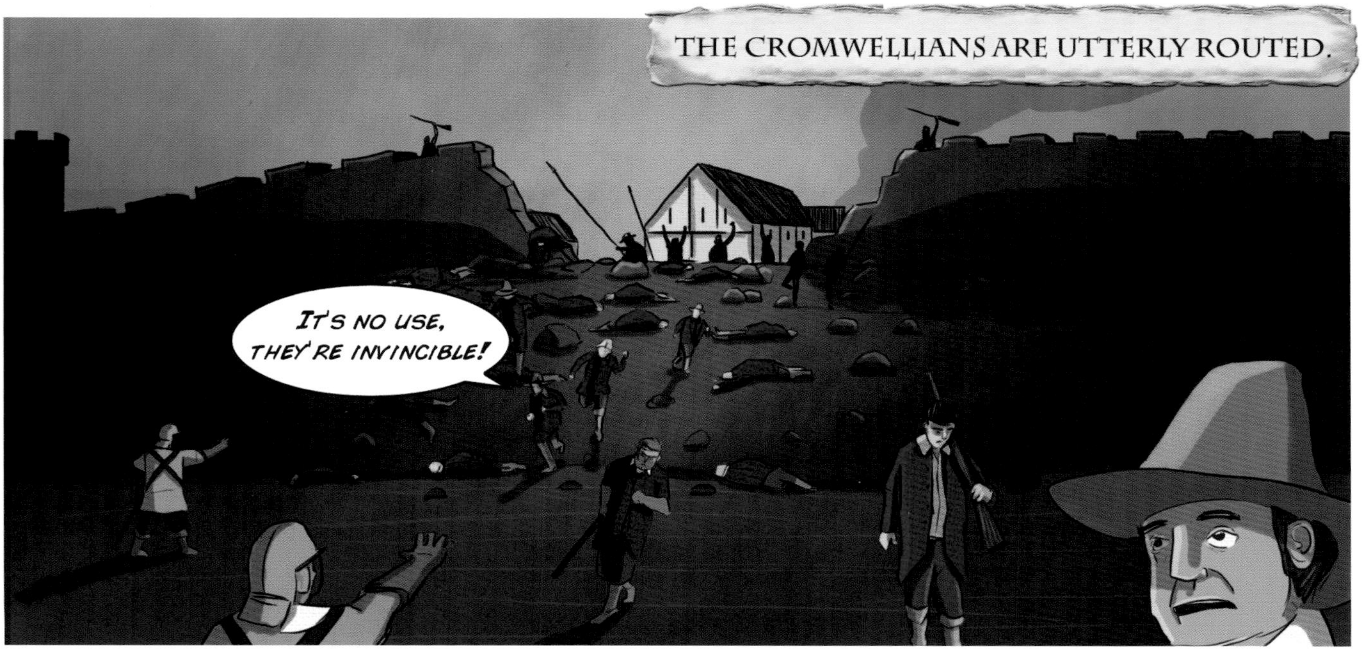
THE CROMWELLIANS ARE UTTERLY ROUTED.
IT'S NO USE, THEY'RE INVINCIBLE!

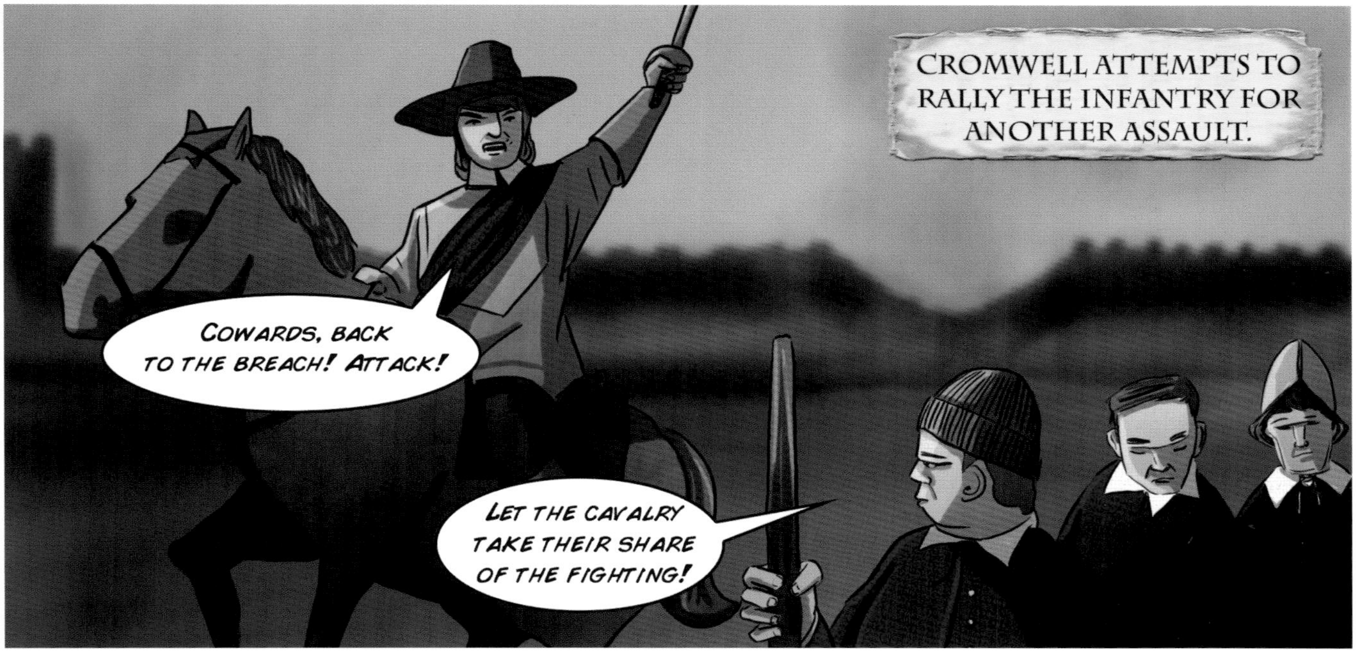
CROMWELL ATTEMPTS TO RALLY THE INFANTRY FOR ANOTHER ASSAULT.
COWARDS, BACK TO THE BREACH! ATTACK!
LET THE CAVALRY TAKE THEIR SHARE OF THE FIGHTING!

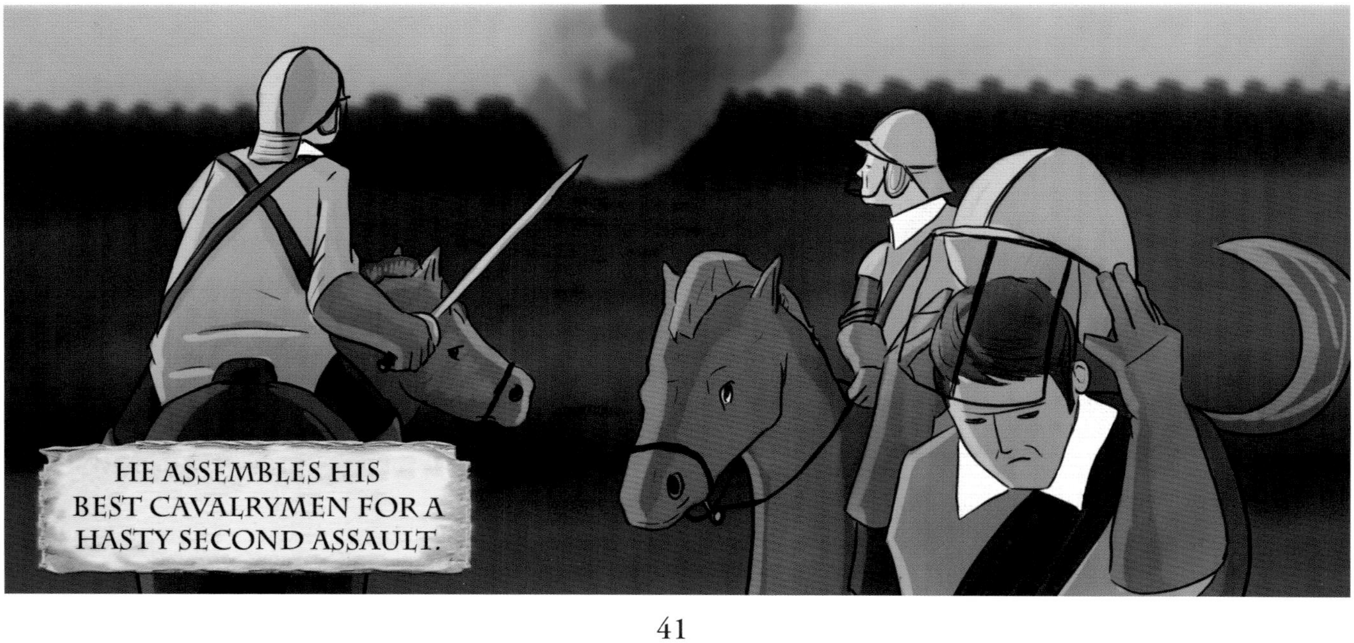
HE ASSEMBLES HIS BEST CAVALRYMEN FOR A HASTY SECOND ASSAULT.

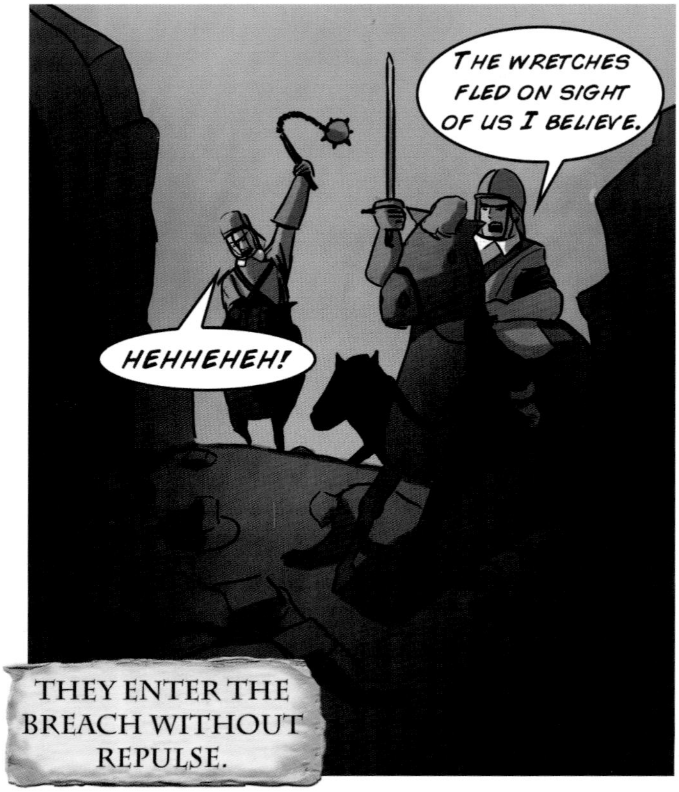
THE WRETCHES FLED ON SIGHT OF US I BELIEVE.
HEHHEHEH!
THEY ENTER THE BREACH WITHOUT REPULSE.

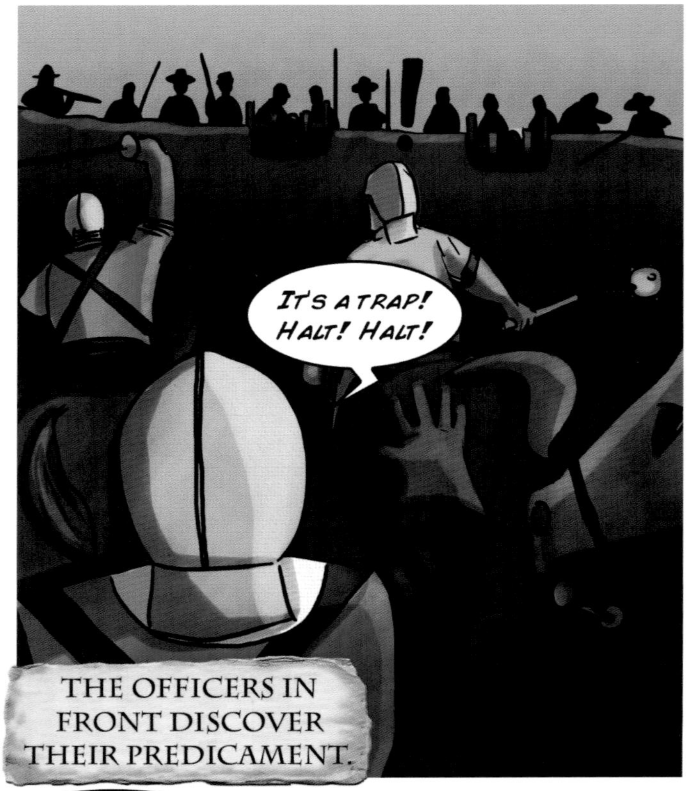
IT'S A TRAP! HALT! HALT!
THE OFFICERS IN FRONT DISCOVER THEIR PREDICAMENT.

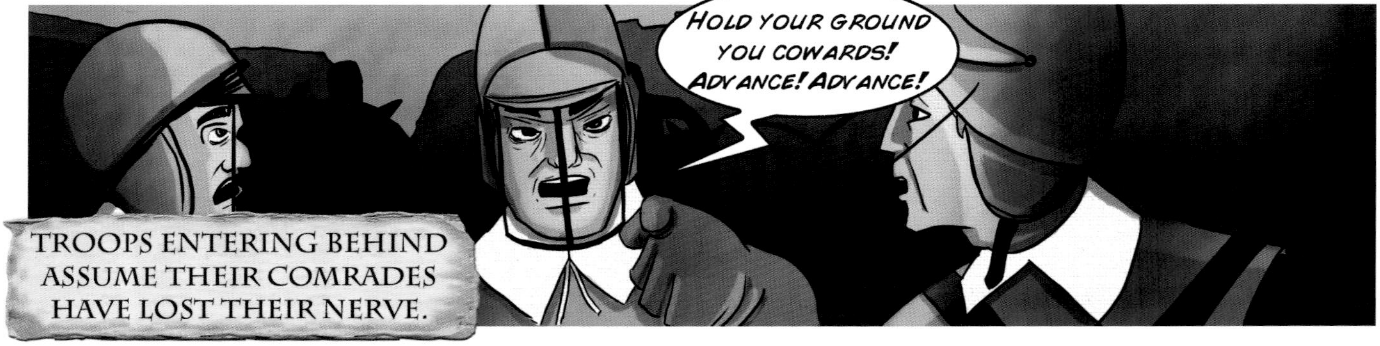
HOLD YOUR GROUND YOU COWARDS! ADVANCE! ADVANCE!
TROOPS ENTERING BEHIND ASSUME THEIR COMRADES HAVE LOST THEIR NERVE.

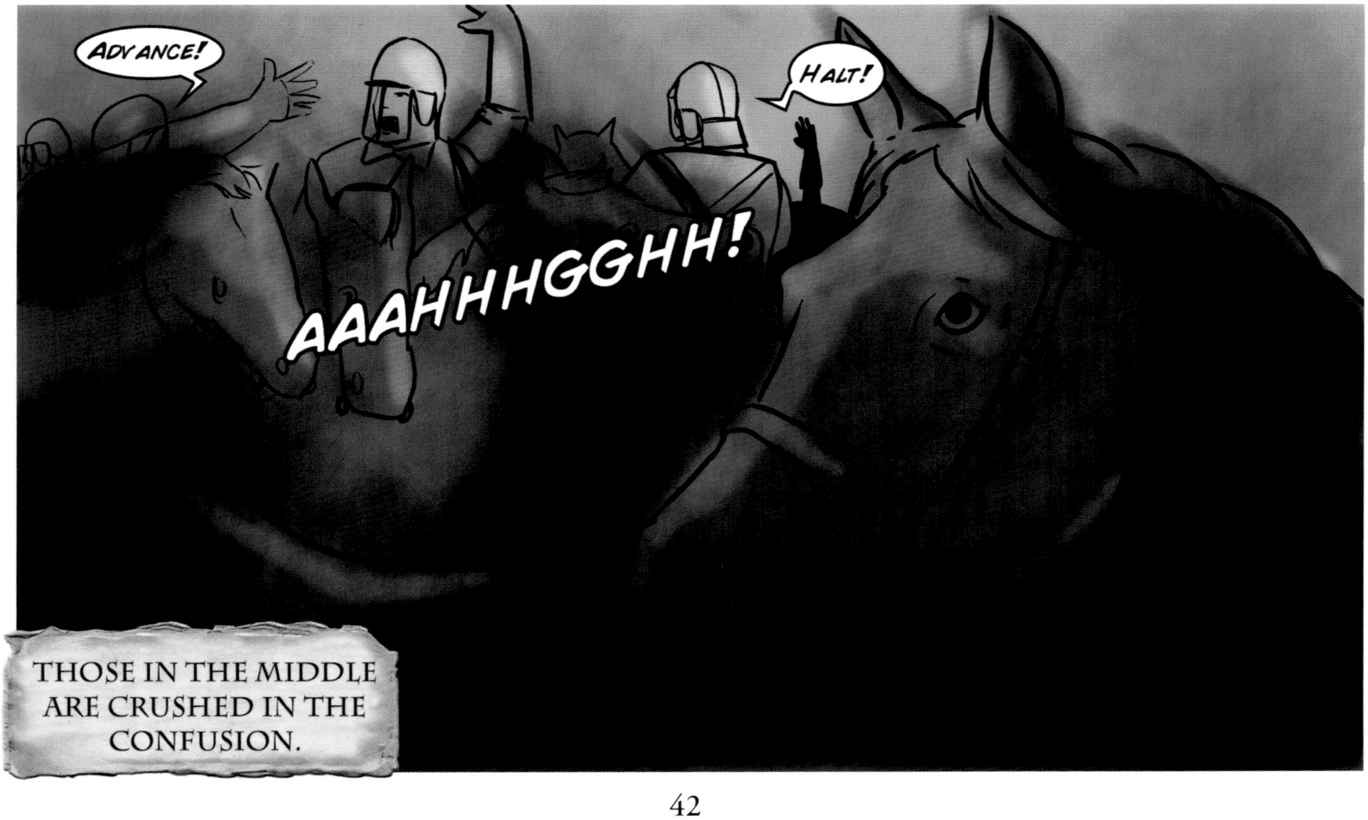
ADVANCE!
HALT!
AAAHHHGGHH!
THOSE IN THE MIDDLE ARE CRUSHED IN THE CONFUSION.

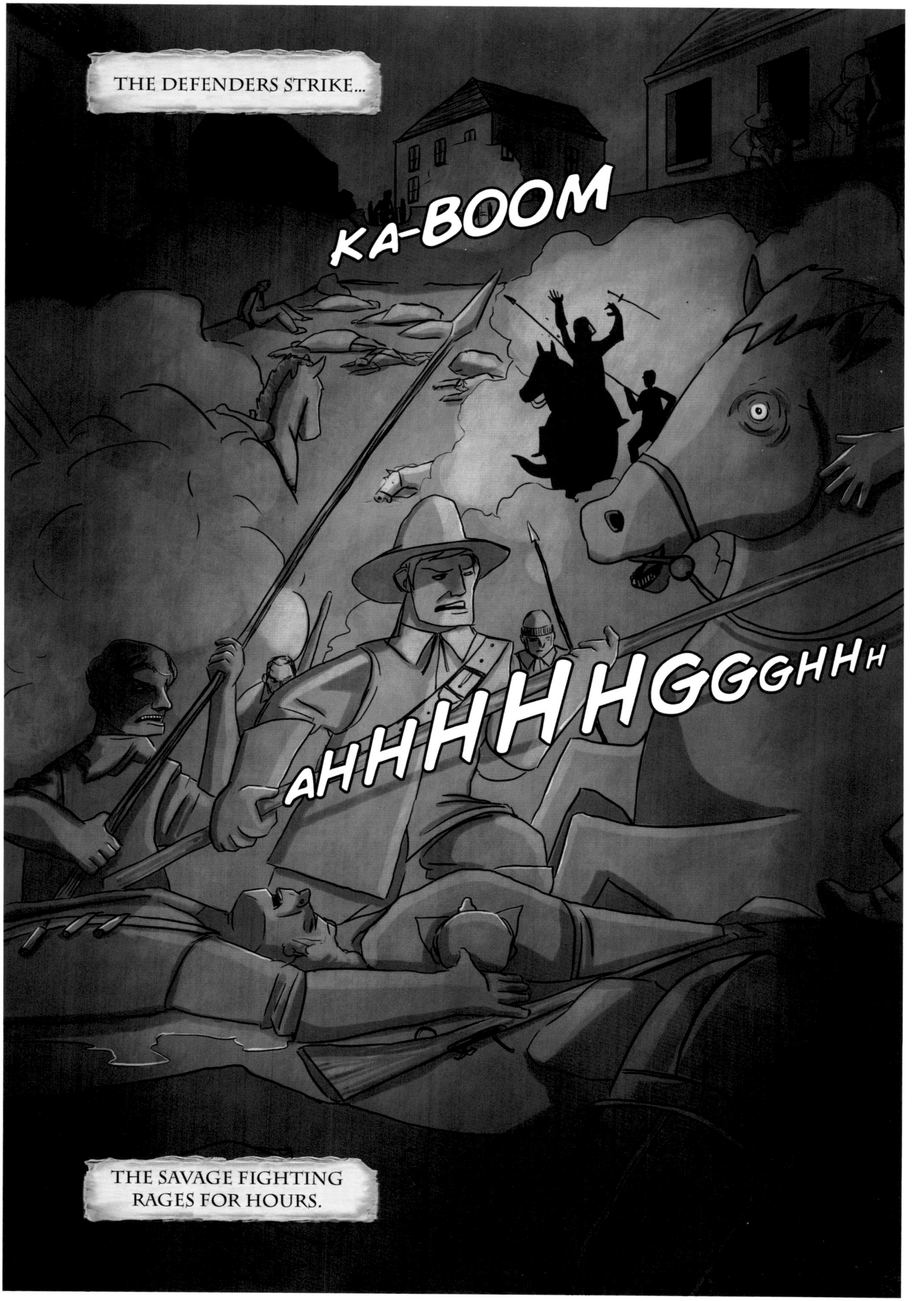
THE DEFENDERS STRIKE...
KA-BOOM
AHHHHHGGGHHH
THE SAVAGE FIGHTING RAGES FOR HOURS.

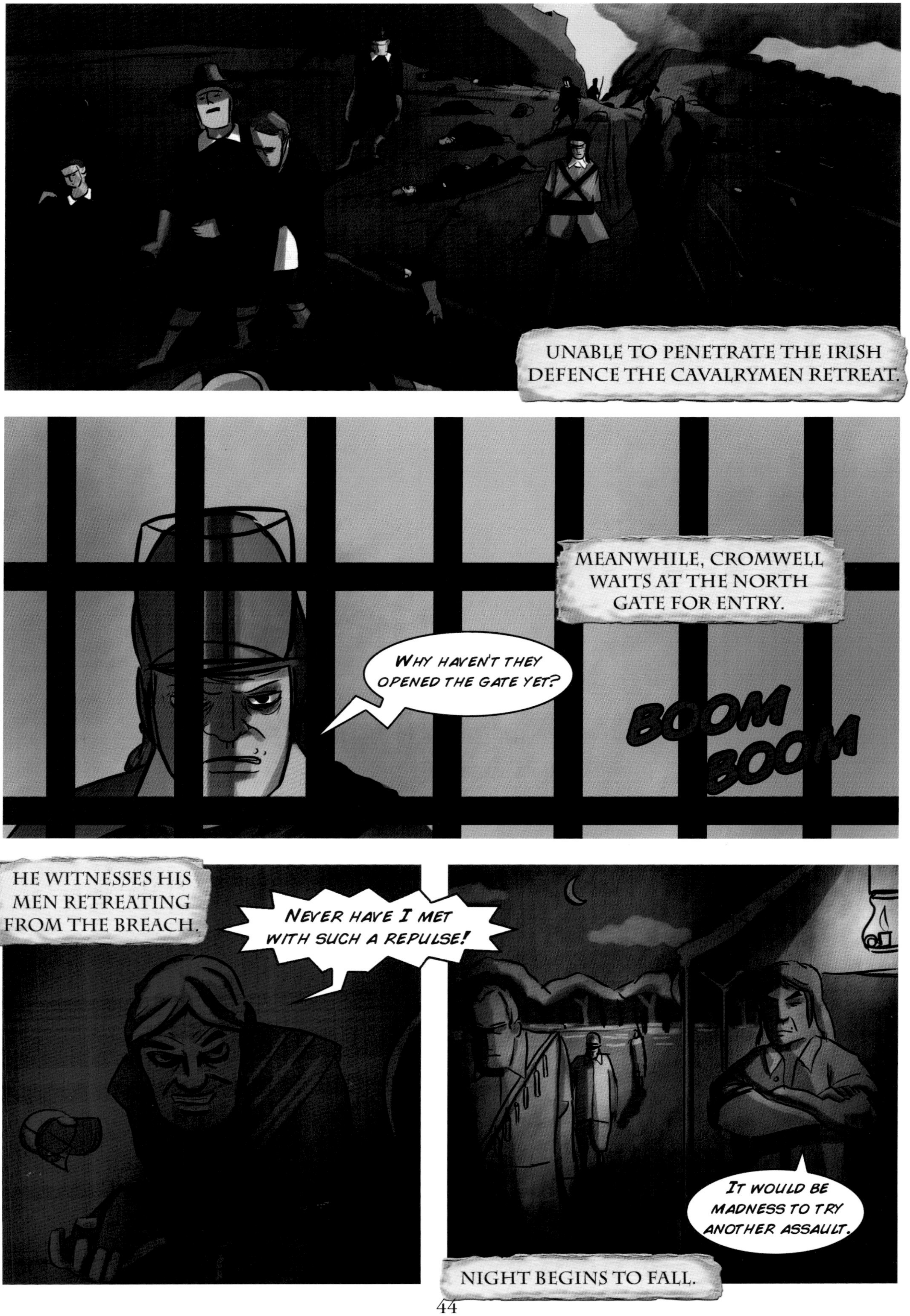
UNABLE TO PENETRATE THE IRISH DEFENCE THE CAVALRYMEN RETREAT.
MEANWHILE, CROMWELL WAITS AT THE NORTH GATE FOR ENTRY.
WHY HAVEN'T THEY OPENED THE GATE YET?
BOOM
BOOM
HE WITNESSES HIS MEN RETREATING FROM THE BREACH.
NEVER HAVE I MET WITH SUCH A REPULSE!
IT WOULD BE MADNESS TO TRY ANOTHER ASSAULT.
NIGHT BEGINS TO FALL.

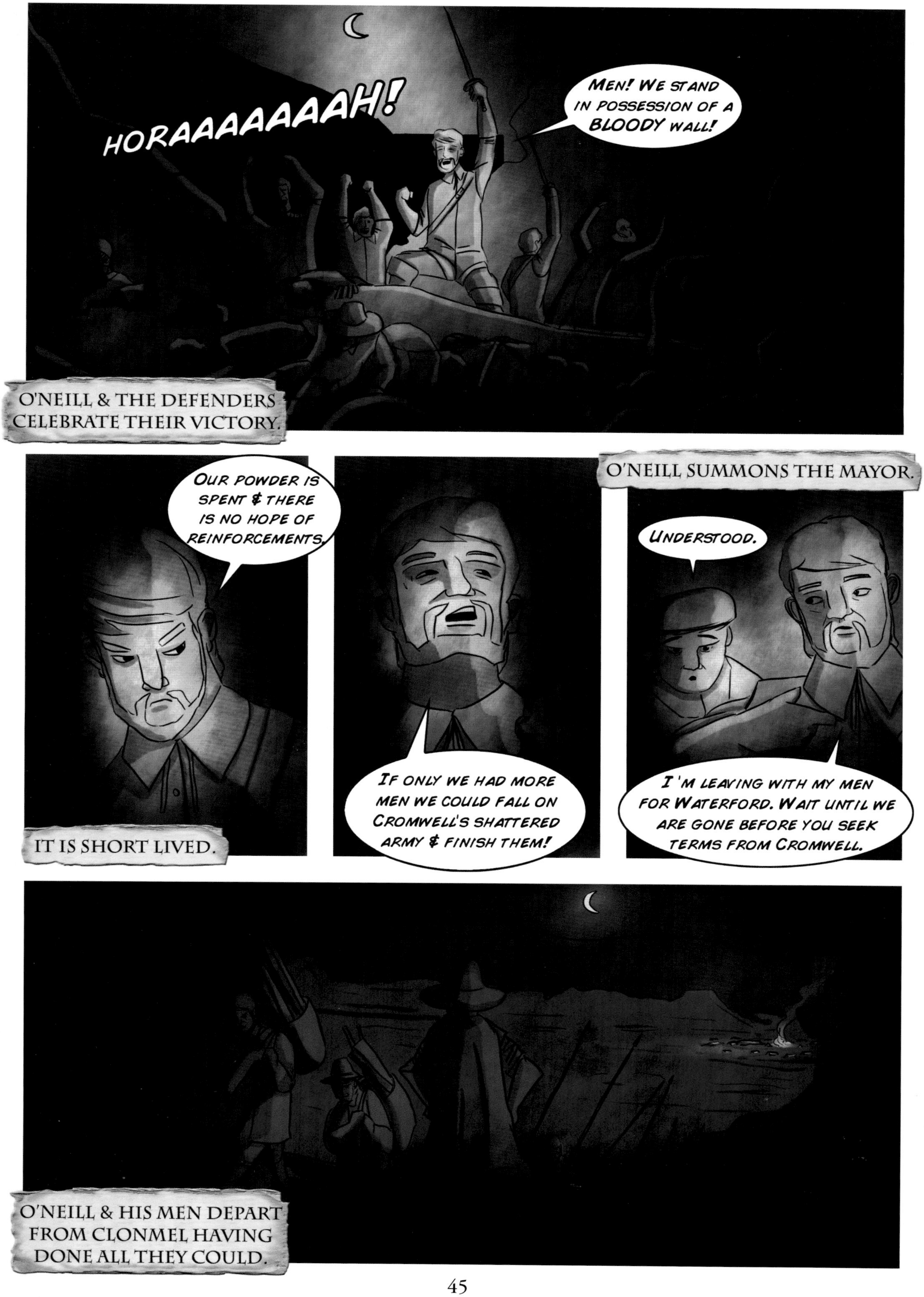
HORAAAAAAAH!
MEN! WE STAND IN POSSESSION OF A BLOODY WALL!
O'NEILL & THE DEFENDERS CELEBRATE THEIR VICTORY.
OUR POWDER IS SPENT & THERE IS NO HOPE OF REINFORCEMENTS.
IT IS SHORT LIVED.
IF ONLY WE HAD MORE MEN WE COULD FALL ON CROMWELL'S SHATTERED ARMY & FINISH THEM!
O'NEILL SUMMONS THE MAYOR.
UNDERSTOOD.
I'M LEAVING WITH MY MEN FOR WATERFORD. WAIT UNTIL WE ARE GONE BEFORE YOU SEEK TERMS FROM CROMWELL.
O'NEILL & HIS MEN DEPART FROM CLONMEL HAVING DONE ALL THEY COULD.

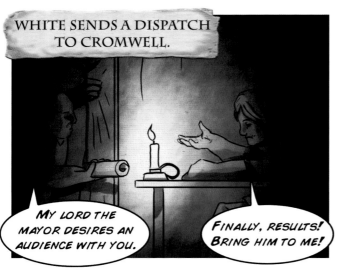

WHITE SENDS A DISPATCH TO CROMWELL.
MY LORD THE MAYOR DESIRES AN AUDIENCE WITH YOU.
FINALLY, RESULTS! BRING HIM TO ME!
THE KEYS TO CLONMEL ARE YOURS PROVIDED YOU GUARANTEE THE LIVES OF THE TOWNSPEOPLE.
VERY WELL, YOU HAVE MY WORD.
DOES O'NEILL KNOW OF YOUR COMING OUT?
O'NEILL LEFT WITH HIS MEN SOME TIME AGO.
YOU KNAVE! HAVE YOU SERVED ME SO, & DID NOT THINK TO TELL ME BEFORE?
IF YOU DEMANDED THE QUESTION OF ME I WOULD HAVE TOLD YOU MY LORD!
I TRUST THE TERMS AGREED STILL STAND?
THEY DO.
TELL ME WHITE, WHO WAS THAT DUFF O'NEILL?
AN OVERSEA SOLDIER BORN IN SPAIN.
GOD DAMN YOU & YOUR OVERSEA! I SWEAR I WILL FOLLOW HIM WHEREVER HE GOES!

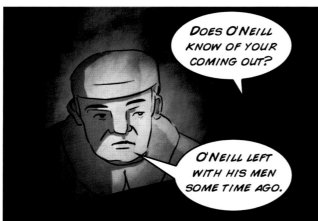

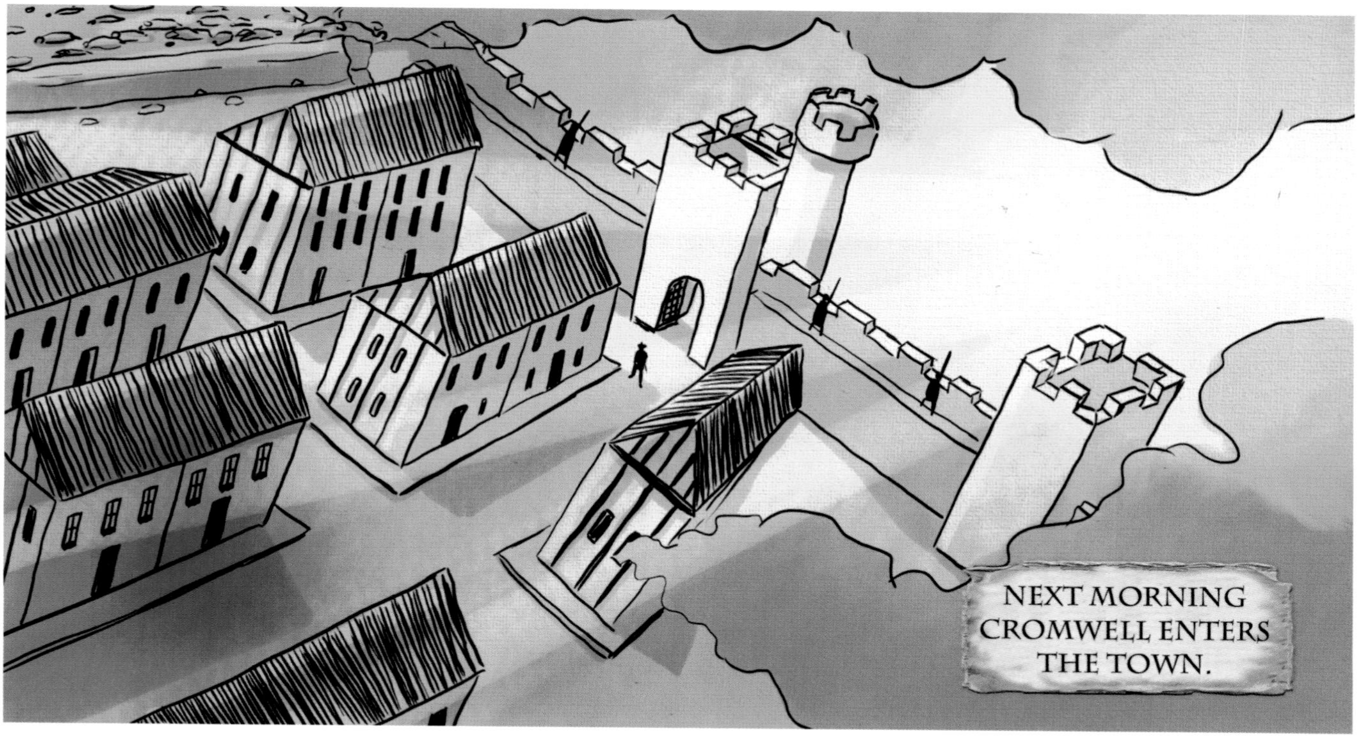
NEXT MORNING
CROMWELL ENTERS
THE TOWN.

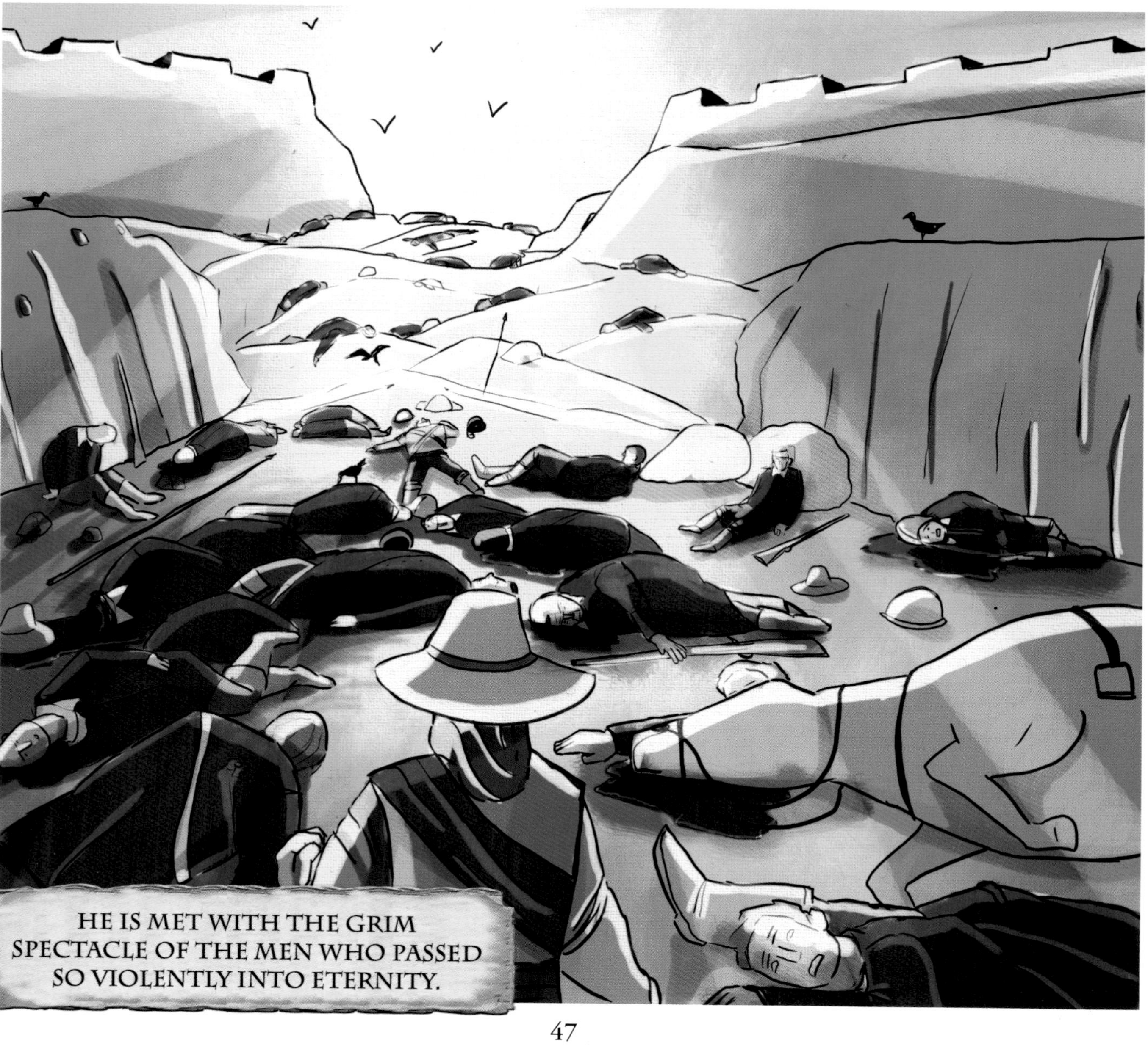
HE IS MET WITH THE GRIM
SPECTACLE OF THE MEN WHO PASSED
SO VIOLENTLY INTO ETERNITY.

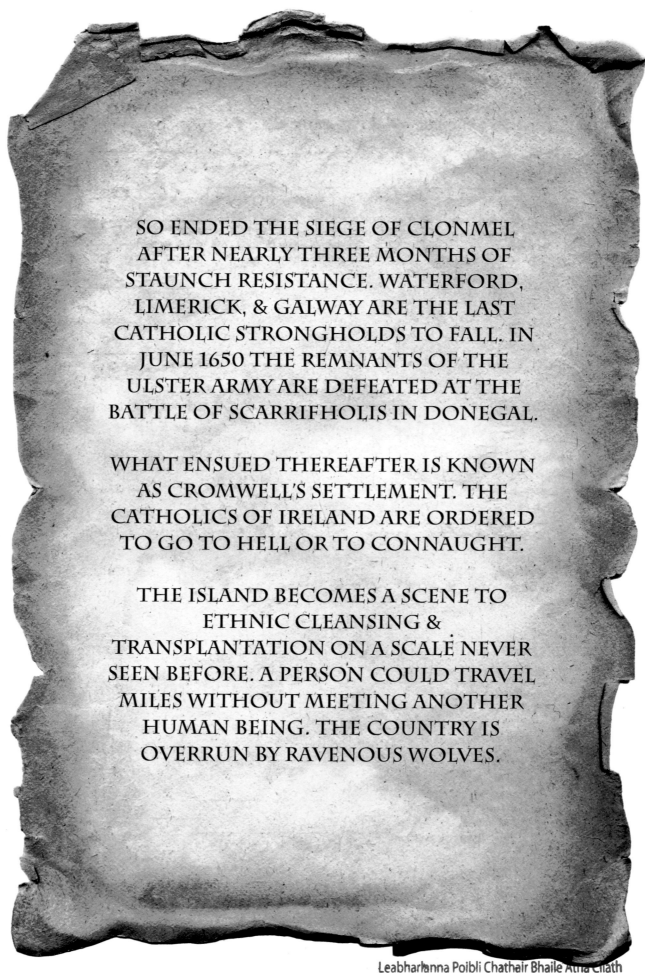

SO ENDED THE SIEGE OF CLONMEL AFTER NEARLY THREE MONTHS OF STAUNCH RESISTANCE. WATERFORD, LIMERICK, & GALWAY ARE THE LAST CATHOLIC STRONGHOLDS TO FALL. IN JUNE 1650 THE REMNANTS OF THE ULSTER ARMY ARE DEFEATED AT THE BATTLE OF SCARRIFHOLIS IN DONEGAL.

WHAT ENSUED THEREAFTER IS KNOWN AS CROMWELL'S SETTLEMENT. THE CATHOLICS OF IRELAND ARE ORDERED TO GO TO HELL OR TO CONNAUGHT.

THE ISLAND BECOMES A SCENE TO ETHNIC CLEANSING & TRANSPLANTATION ON A SCALE NEVER SEEN BEFORE. A PERSON COULD TRAVEL MILES WITHOUT MEETING ANOTHER HUMAN BEING. THE COUNTRY IS OVERRUN BY RAVENOUS WOLVES.